PRAISE FOR
HIDING HOPE

"Linni Weishaar is a gifted writer and wounded healer. In *Hiding Hope*, she openly invites the reader into her unashamed brokenness as the great bridge to reach others in need of restoration.

This book exhibits restored hope, authentic forgiveness, genuine love—by any means necessary—and Linni's freedom is infectious! Blessed is Linni who believed, for there will be fulfillment of those things which were told to her from the Lord."

Tegra Little, Founder and President at No Longer Bound Abortion and Miscarriage Recovery Ministry, author of *No Longer Bound: The Unborn Children*

"When life throws you a curve ball, it takes resilience, determination, and hope to continue walking by faith and not by sight. In her book *Hiding Hope*, Linni Weishaar shares her personal story—and her faith in the sure promises of God—in the face of deep challenges, loss, and God-given miracles.

With candidness and transparency, she takes you on a journey to walk closer to Jesus through every twist and turn on life's path.

Read this book and receive a fresh revelation of God's promise for your life: *'Now may the God of hope fill you with all joy and peace in believing, so that you will abound in hope by the power of the Holy Spirit'* (Romans 15:13)."

Dr. Ché Ahn, Senior Pastor at Harvest Rock Church, Pasadena, CA, President at Harvest International Ministry, International Chancellor at Wagner University

"Linni Weishaar, in her book *Hiding Hope*, gracefully captures her reader with encounters that truly draw you into her journey and which convey the depth of her emotions associated with loss, grief, disappointment, fear, brokenness, and despair.

Yet, simultaneously, and ultimately, she brings the reader out on the other side of her journey with a testimony of deep inner freedom, increased hope, faith, and love.

May this book and Linni's journey serve as a catalyst for other women who can identify with the loss of a child through a miscarriage, abortion, or otherwise, or the loss of hope of ever having a child. May it be a source of inspiration for other women to take steps of faith, to find the healing available in a genuinely caring community, through ministries such as No Longer Bound.

May our Heavenly Father use both this story and Linni's life, as a gifted group facilitator and ambassador for Christ, calling other women into freedom in the days and years to come!"

Roxanne Jordan, M.Div., Psy.D., Senior Vice President of Programs & Clinical Services at the Los Angeles Mission

HIDING
HOPE

A JOURNEY OF FAITH THROUGH
INFERTILITY, MISCARRIAGES,
AND MIRACLE BABIES

HIDING
HOPE

a memoir

LINNI WEISHAAR

GALEA
PRESS

*Hiding Hope: A Journey of Faith Through Infertility, Miscarriages, and
Miracle Babies*

Copyright © 2023 by Linni Weishaar

www.LinniWeishaar.com

All rights reserved. No part of this book may be reproduced in any form
without written permission from the author.

Disclaimer: This book is not meant to be a substitute for professional
medical advice and treatment from your own doctor or to offer medical
or psychological guidance. People who are contemplating suicide or who
have experienced emotional, physical, or sexual abuse ought to get
assistance from a mental health specialist or qualified therapist.

The publisher, the author, and each ministry mentioned disclaim all
liability for any conceivable outcomes of any action done by anyone who
reads or heeds the content in this book. The author writes from her own
experience and does not advise following her steps, unless approved by
a healthcare professional.

Scriptures taken from the Holy Bible, New International Version®,
NIV®. Copyright © 1973, 1978, 1984, 2011 by Biblica, Inc.™ Used by
permission of Zondervan. All rights reserved worldwide.
www.zondervan.com The "NIV" and "New International Version" are
trademarks registered in the United States Patent and Trademark
Office by Biblica, Inc.™

Cover and Interior design by Rachel Rasmussen and Linni Weishaar

Image: Vintage Book Cover 2 by Clint Cearly (courtesy of Shutterstock,
Stock Photo ID: 7273639)

Library of Congress Cataloging-in-Publication Data Weishaar, Linni.
*Hiding Hope: A Journey of Faith Through Infertility, Miscarriages, and
Miracle Babies* / Linni Weishaar. —1st edition.
    ISBN 979-8-218-14665-8 (print)
    1. Spirituality 2. Religion 3. Memoir

Printed in the United States of America
10 9 8 7 6 5 4 3 2 1

To my beloved husband, thank you for helping me retire my superhero cape.

To my late mama, thank you for leaving an inheritance of faith to the next generation. Your grandchildren now carry on your legacy.

To my children: Claire, Mia, Daniel, Aurora, Mikayla, Gavin, Alyssa, Dylan, Victoria, and Noelle, you are bone of my bone and flesh of my flesh. Each of you have a place and purpose in eternity. You are loved more than words could ever express. I carried each of you for every second of your life, and I will love you for every second of mine.

PREFACE

Life is full of unexpected twists and turns that can take us down paths we never anticipated.

At times, we may find ourselves walking through the valley of the shadow of death, where darkness and despair surround us at every turn. Where Psalm 23 becomes more and more real with each passing day.

The valley is a place where hope feels lost and the weight of our struggles can seem too much to bear. Yet in this journey, we have an invitation to discover that it can also be where our faith grows rooted in an unshakeable God, where we learn to have sheer determination that pain won't be the end of our story, and where supernatural healing from Jesus Christ can take place.

I originally wrote portions of *Hiding Hope* as a blog years ago when blogs were popular. I was writing to process my hope and my pain in real-time with friends who lived across the country. What I didn't expect was for the blog to be shared reaching Europe, Africa, and throughout the United States.

I received emails from people all over the world

who had never experienced my specific kind of journey but were resonating with it. Grief and loss, hope and faith are a unifying language of connection.

It simultaneously thrilled me and terrified me that my story was spreading as it was unfolding. But I wasn't ready to minister to that capacity, in the midst of my journey, so I shut it down.

After allowing my heart to marinate in healing, good friends encouraged me to write again. So, here is my story—my full story of how Jesus took me from death to life and poured the oil of gladness over my head.

Whether you are currently navigating your own valley or seeking to support someone who is, may this book serve as an inspiration and hope that if you're going through Hell, God isn't done with your story just yet. There is healing on the other side of the valley.

THE DAY MY HEART STOPPED

"Fetal demise."

The doctor said it coldly as she walked out of the exam room. The door slowly closed behind her. The latch clicked into place.

I stared at Craig, my husband of two years. No emotion detected on his face. I was still wrapped in my medical blanket, lying on the white paper with my bare feet on the cold stirrups, as her words began to register in my mind.

No heartbeat. Heart-shaped uterus, ten percent chance of ever having children.

The world stood still. My heart stopped. My mind went blank. I would never be a mama.

What? I would never be a mama?

The question repeated in my mind. I wanted to yell out. Cry. React. Nothing came out. My voice was silent. Darkness crept in and held my voice captive. This was our third miscarriage in two years.

I slid off the table, put on my jeans and slipped on my sandals. I opened the door to face the nurses' station. One nurse was on the phone with the facility's ultrasound technician, scheduling an appointment to see if a higher-resolution machine could detect the heartbeat of our baby.

I felt nothing. *Shock.*

How could this be? How could I be a woman and not have a working uterus? How could three miscarriages mean infertility?

Questions whirled around my head, but I couldn't will myself to say anything.

Later that night, I lay on another exam table with another technician. It was confirmed. Heart-shaped, bicornuate uterus. No heartbeat.

My baby stopped growing at five weeks. I was supposed to be seven and a half weeks along. No reason was given.

Craig and I drove home in silence.

I did the only thing I knew how to do. Plow ahead. I went to work the next day. I still had morning sickness or all-day sickness in my case. I worked my tail off trying to keep my mind from going dark.

How unfair. My 23-year-old body thinks I'm pregnant. This morning sickness means nothing.

False hope. I couldn't rely on symptoms to let me know that my baby was growing. Now it was an anxiety-ridden waiting game to see if I would miscarry naturally or have a D&C.

I kept hearing the doctor's voice say, *"Ten percent chance of ever having children,"* on repeat in my mind, but deep down, I knew Jesus loved working with those kinds of numbers.

Even so, all my dreams of becoming a mama were crashing around me. I painted a smile on my face as an artist would paint a canvas. I did not have any other tools for coping except to pretend that I was okay on the outside and pray to God for help on the inside.

When I was done with my shift, I sat in my car. I put the keys in the ignition and slowly backed out of my parking space. My phone rang. A longtime friend was calling me. We had not spoken since January, seven months earlier. She lived in Michigan, and I lived in California.

I picked up the phone. "Hey, Rachel."

"Hey," she said. "Listen, God told me you are not supposed to believe what that doctor told you. You will have a baby."

"What?" I yelped. "How did you know what the doctor said? How did you know about the diagnosis yesterday?"

"I didn't. You were on my heart. The Lord told me to call you. You will have a baby, and don't believe what those doctors said, okay?"

I pulled over on the side of the road with hot tears streaming down my face, clouding my vision.

Psalm 23:1-3 — "The Lord is my Shepard, I lack nothing. He makes me to lie down in green pastures and leads me by quiet waters He refreshes my soul. "

I knew God had just promised me a baby. A seed of hope was hidden away, close to my heart. Little did I know that the path I was on would lead me into an unknown fog, where I could no longer see my steps.

"I will walk by faith and not by sight" from 2 Corinthians 5:7 would be my verse from Jesus to cling to for years to come.

Naming a Promise

I raced home with the news. I was given a promise for a baby, and we weren't supposed to believe what the doctor had said the day before.

I ran up the stairs to our little apartment, flung open the door shouting, "We're going to have a baby!"

Craig, a little startled by my exclamation, spun around on the couch.

"What?"

I could barely catch my breath from crying to tell him that we had just been promised a baby. He stood up and held me tightly in his arms until the full story rushed out of my mouth.

He responded with more faith than anyone I knew and said, "If the baby is a girl, we need to pick a name for this promised baby." (If the baby were a boy, we would follow my family's tradition of naming the baby boy after both grandfathers.)

His eyes scanned our bookshelf and found our little blue baby-name book. We hovered over the pages, searching through each section.

"We need a name that means praise. We need to

praise our God. He moves in our praises," Craig kept repeating, determined to find a name.

We skimmed each line for a name that matched our desire to praise God. We found a name that in Hebrew means, "Who is like the Lord?"

We were confident that God would respond to our praises. Who else could give us a baby but our God? We had no idea what a powerful weapon praise would be. Little did we know what praising our God would do for our souls.

Psalm 22:3, 22 — "Yet you are enthroned as the Holy One; you are the one Israel praises…. I will declare your name to my people; in the assembly I will praise you."

Little did we know that our lives would start to feel like one big psalm, one minute asking where God was in our anguish, and the next minute praising Him for his ever-present refuge.

Praise would be our new weapon of choice.

I will choose to praise Him in my darkness; I will choose to praise Him in my joy.

My roller coaster of emotions was just beginning. I prayed for our promised baby, "Bring this baby soon, Lord."

HOPE
INFUSED

Beyond a shadow of a doubt, God spoke. I praised my heart out, hiding in joy, thanking Him for this baby that was not yet in our arms. The next couple of days, I lived on the high of a promise believed.

Then without any warning, I fell into the depths of despair over losing our three babies. I just wanted to hide under the blankets of my bed and never see the light of day again. I didn't understand my emotions—the ensuing hopelessness. I didn't understand my body—the physical pain of my uterus contracting. I didn't understand this was grieving.

Even still, I willed myself out of bed in the midst of my extreme darkness. I dressed for church with determination. I knew that my praise to God wasn't based on my circumstances but on His character. If I really believed that God uses all of us and that He loves me, then I was willing to be used no matter what that cost.

The worship music began, and I raised my hands in the air. If this was a battle, I was going to win it by hiding in praise.

He is good. He is faithful. He is not Santa Claus. He is not a distant deity. He is my Father, and I am his daughter. I'm going to worship Him for that alone.

I cried my eyes out before the Lord. I felt alive with the music. I didn't have a care in the world over who saw my tears. But when the music stopped, I fell back into despair. The service ended. I made a beeline for my friend Bethany.

I confided in her that my miscarriage had started and that my sorrow was deep.

I whispered, "God promised us a baby. I don't understand why I feel so much darkness."

She compassionately and gently said, "You just need to have hope."

Hope. I needed hope! That word was an arrow to my heart. A fresh spring of water in my desert. Yes! I had a promise.

I was going to praise Him even when I didn't feel like it, but I also needed hope that when God speaks, He speaks to accomplish.

Isaiah 55:11 — "[S]o is my word that goes out from my mouth: it will not return to me empty, but will accomplish what I desire and achieve the purpose for which I sent it."

Just four days after our infertility diagnosis, HOPE was infused within the depths of my soul as if it was hiding in a secret garden. We picked the middle name for our future miracle baby: Hope.

A HEART'S ROLLER COASTER

I did not understand my own emotional roller coaster. One on hand, I would talk about our promise of a baby and on the other, I would talk about my miscarried babies being gone, wishing at some point my external processing would articulate a solution for my broken heart.

I would call Rachel, bawling my eyes out. Her response every time was, "God told me you're going to have a baby."

I needed that reminder constantly because it seemed impossible to believe this promise would come as the months dragged on.

Psalm 13:1 — "How long, LORD? Will you forget me forever? How long will you hide your face from me?"

I simultaneously had hope and despair. I was in the desert, walking towards the hope of an oasis. Yet a dark cloud hovered over me. I had God, but my arms were empty. I had my husband, but he didn't understand my turmoil. My heartache was my own burden to carry.

We had chromosomal testing and bloodwork done on the tissue of our miscarried baby. Everything came back normal.

I felt like someone smashed my heart in with a hammer and then kicked it into the gutter for good measure. Even still, I had a glimmer of hope at moments.

My mom flew me home to Ohio for two weeks. I sat in her bed with her arms wrapped around me. My mother-in-law was also compassionate towards me, calling me often. A few close friends tried to console me. I knew I was a walking conundrum. I could be comforted momentarily, but it didn't last long most days. Yet, I still hung onto a hidden hope that I wouldn't be in despair forever.

As an avid reader, I loved books, but I couldn't find any on infertility and miscarriages that brought me comfort. Most books I read could be simply summarized as:

"Miscarriages are hard, but God is good."

Not comforting at all. I wanted to read a book that showed the space between the *comma* and the *but*. The space that showed me the journey of pain and suffering with God in the midst, not just the euphoric sentiment that "God made me whole, now I'm fine, and you'll be fine, too."

I would come to find out that books on grieving the death of a loved one were more appropriate in describing my darkness than any book on a miscarriage.

It was a mental balancing act of emotions. I could not seem to keep it steady. Even Craig had a hard time understanding my emotional roller coaster. I didn't know how to communicate the depths of darkness that threatened to overrun me. I was bound.

The advice started coming in from the older ladies in our little church.

One Sunday morning, a church lady came over to me and said, "Just make sure you are grieving the correct way."

I wish I had said, "What in the world do you mean by that? Are you saying God is offended by my emotions?"

The idea to speak up against such advice didn't come to me. I silently accepted the admonishment.

After another lady gave me a scripture verse to memorize, she couldn't understand why I wasn't happy again. "Well, didn't you memorize that verse?" she questioned me incredulously.

My lips didn't move. Apparently, I needed a step-by-step, formulaic plan to receive God's comfort.

If only it was that easy.

She must have overlooked how Job cried out to God, asking Him if He forgot that he was made of just a breath.

I had no idea how to respond to their strict, religious to-do lists and advice that had no room for emotions or questions. I was not raised on empty, religious sentiments. I was raised in a house of prayer and declarations of healing. Their advice came faster than their prayers.

Since, I couldn't find a book on miscarriages that

brought me any understanding as to why I was so distraught, I started to find solace in the books of Job and Psalms.

Job 7:7 — "Remember, O God, that my life is but a breath; my eyes will never see happiness again."

When I was alone, I looked at Job and saw that God restored his family to him *after* he prayed for his friends. When I was on the brink of despair, I looked at King David and saw that God delivered him *while* he praised God in the midst of his heartache.

I read the Bible from cover to cover, searching for stories where God reached out His hand to the downtrodden. I discovered that is God's specialty.

How to Build an Altar

Deep down, I wanted to believe my eyes would see happiness again. God reaches out His hand to the distraught. I knew this was true. I didn't want to forget it.

I needed a physical reminder of the promise of a baby that was yet to be fulfilled. I needed a resting place in my time of waiting. I needed a quiet place to calm my weary soul. If this place existed, I was going to find it. The hunt was on.

I loved reading about the practice of building altars to God in the Old Testament as an act of worship. When the Israelites would start to forget God's faithfulness, His miracles, they needed a place to go back to, a reminder of a time when God proved Himself faithful.

After God parted the Jordan River, the Israelites built an altar. When the Israelites defeated the Philistines against all odds, they built an altar. When God showed Himself to Jacob in a dream, Jacob built an altar as a way for future generations to remember what God had done and the promises of His faithfulness.

Mark Batterson, in his book, *Wild Goose Chase*, says, "Altars help us remember what God doesn't want us to forget. The altar was a place of worship and remembrance of when God showed up and did a miracle."

I needed a miracle. God was already showing up in my despair. I wanted an altar—a physical reminder of this promise that my arms would one day be full.

I scoured the internet and found my idea of a modern-day altar: a black, nursery rocking chair.

This was a significant part of my spiritual walk of faith. What sane person buys a rocking chair without a baby to rock?

Apparently, *me*, that's who.

At the time, it felt like the craziest idea I ever had. Sorrow has a way of doing that to you.

This black wooden rocking chair became my new resting place, my calm in the storm, and my place of refuge when all medical options seemed impossible. It was my refuge when I needed still and calm to remind myself that God is bigger than all of my fears and doubts. When I needed a tangible reminder that I was not alone in this journey, I would rock in my rocking chair with my Bible in my arms and worship music playing in my ear.

It was in that chair, clinging to Jesus, that I prayed for Mikayla Hope as if she were already in my arms. It would be two more years and another baby lost before I would hold Mikayla Hope's little pink body in my arms while sitting in my place of remembrance.

ONE WAY TO RUIN A PARTY

I had a friend who was due a few days after what would have been the birth of my own baby. We had told each other simultaneously, "I'm pregnant!" months earlier.

I watched my friend's belly grow each month as I had one negative pregnancy test after another. I prayed for her in her living room. I prayed from afar for her, too. I didn't want anything to happen to that baby. I wanted that baby to be placed in her arms. I needed to know that someone could be happy.

Her baby shower was just around the corner. When the invitation arrived, I responded, "Yes." I desperately wanted to be a good friend. I wanted to show how truly happy I was for her. I wanted to be supportive. I thought I would be okay.

But as I approached the front door of the house, I felt like an internal shipwreck. I was drowning. I was caught completely off guard by my emotions. I thought I was starting to heal from my sorrow, but now I realized I was underwater.

I made a mistake. I shouldn't have come.

I took a deep breath and pulled my (proverbial) companion out of my back pocket. My trusty little friend was named, the "I'm great!" mask.

I rang the doorbell, and a woman answered. "How are you?" she asked.

"I'm great!" the mask replied.

"Come on in. Isn't this exciting?"

"Yes, it is!" the mask said, matching the woman's joyous tone.

I admired the living room. The space was decorated with blue streamers and balloons. Blue baby-boy onesies were strung on a clothesline over the picture window. Blue desserts and blueberry lemonade were placed on the table. The house was straight out of a magazine. It was truly beautiful.

Soon the blueness started to taunt me. I would have had a shower too...possibly that same weekend. My friend and I could have easily switched places. Although I didn't want her in my shoes, I desperately wanted to be in hers.

I nestled in between two other women on the couch, gaining my composure. The mask settled into place. Gifts were unwrapped and passed around for all to admire, a never-ending assembly line of beautiful baby items paraded in front of me.

Suddenly, without warning, the air grew hot. The room was closing in around me. I didn't know how much longer the mask would stay in place. Panic enveloped me.

As soon as the last gift was oohed and aahed over by each woman, I made up an excuse to leave early, hoping I wasn't ruining the baby shower. I couldn't breathe. The mask was starting to disintegrate. I hid my tears behind my dark sunglasses as I closed the door on the bubbling party of fertility.

I breathed a sigh of relief that I had escaped without ruining her special moment. I rushed to my car.

As I started the engine, the Lord's peace encompassed me. Tears streamed down my face. I felt His love for me. The panic attack ceased.

Psalm 119:76a — "May your unfailing love be my comfort..."

WE ALL NEED A CHEERLEADER

My due date came and went. The sorrow had lessened, but I desperately wanted to know what was wrong with my body.

Determination filled me. I was going to figure out why I kept miscarrying.

Being diagnosed with a heart-shaped, bicornuate uterus meant there was no cure. No reconstructive surgery could help. I'm not sure why, but I was starting to doubt if I really did have a bicornuate uterus.

Trying to get a second opinion was harder than I thought it would be. I called countless doctors for hormonal bloodwork, ultrasounds, or anything else that could be done within my health insurance provider's network and referrals. All dead ends.

I needed a secretary for problem solving doctor and insurance issues. It was a time-consuming mess. Calling doctors and waiting for their callbacks was an infuriating task. Playing phone tag with medical offices was not my idea of fun.

I was losing hope that Mikayla Hope would ever

come. We needed someone with expertise in this field to believe with us that we would have a baby.

My mom, who was my biggest cheerleader, took on the job of secretary-researcher. It seemed she had more faith than I did that I would have a baby. She told me often that if God said I was going to have a baby, I was going to have a baby. End of story.

Her hope in God breathed life into my dry bones. I clung to her words of hope, wishing she was right, but secretly thinking, *What if she's wrong?*

Dr. Brené Brown, a researcher out of the University of Houston, says in her book, *Daring Greatly*, that hope is a learned behavior. I saw my mom cling to Jesus with hope when she experienced her own health problems as I was growing up. Holding onto hope was not a foreign concept to me.

My mom was diagnosed with multiple sclerosis (MS) when I was three years old. She had her fair share of doctors telling her there was nothing they could do. The phrase "Go home and live with it," said by one doctor, sent my mom straight out of the medical community and around the world in search of alternative ways to cure her MS all through my formative years. In her opinion, a ten percent chance of ever having children was still a good chance, and there was no reason for me to give up believing that God still does miracles.

I was raised watching her fight a disease that took away her body—a slow death of her nervous system. She truly believed she would be healed, even as she was bedridden, a prisoner in her own body. Little did I know how much her fight to find a cure would be motivation for us to keep on trying for a baby.

A few days after my mama took charge of researching fertility specialists for me, she found a midwife in our area who specialized in infertility. She was willing to see me! I was beyond excited. After months of dead ends and closed doors within the traditional medical community, I had a window of possibility!

> *2 Samuel 22:29 — "You, LORD, are*
> *my lamp; the LORD turns my*
> *darkness into light."*

The moment that darkness, hopelessness, and blackness detect a ray of sunshine, the world turns right-side-up inside one's soul. The tiniest ray of light had fallen onto my darkened path. My soul was made upright by this new opportunity to see the midwife. I was ready to try anything. Anything at all. I had a new pep in my step.

Hope was rising again—the kind of hope that is not an emotion, but an expectation with certainty that God would fulfill His promise.

THE LAND OF
HOPE

I pulled open the lobby door to the midwife's waiting room. The decor was in a time warp between the 1970s and the Victorian era. This was not the typical doctor's office I was expecting. I felt my excitement quickly turn into anxiety.

Deep maroon curtains with gold tassels darkened both the windows and the room, while worn maroon carpet covered the floors. There was no overhead lighting. A few floor lamps were placed in each corner. The wood paneling was orange in color. The walls were lined with dark, ornately cushioned armchairs.

I was apprehensive about going this alternative route, but since so many other doors had been closed within the traditional medical community, this seemed to be the best option. Waiting with nervous anticipation, Craig and I found two armchairs side-by-side and sat down.

The midwife's assistant called my name. We slowly made our way down the hall to her office.

The door to one room was ajar on the right. I stole a glance into the room as I walked by. A sagging queen-size bed, reminiscent of an old hotel, was in the middle of the room.

Wow, this is so not normal. We have arrived in granola land. Women actually have babies in these beds without an epidural! Imagine that!

I was completely out of my comfort zone.

What in the world did my mom get me into?!

We waited in the office with a pink exam table next to the orange, wood-paneled wall. The midwife finally glided into the room. She was a fiery redhead with a personality to match.

Oh, my mama is gonna like you.

I was enveloped by her confidence. I liked her immediately. She had been a midwife forever. My momentary fears of this being a crazy idea dissipated. She was sure of herself, and I wanted that personality trait on this journey.

I desired confidence. I didn't care anymore if her method wasn't the typical way of doing things. I was ready to do anything.

I loved how much she listened. It was the first time someone listened to me for more than three seconds. I wasn't rushed. Her listening to me made me feel like a real person for the first time in a long time.

This midwife's specialty was making me feel comfortable...maybe even powerful.

I was no longer a nameless patient or a number on a chart. I had a name. A story. Feelings. I was sold. She was going to hold my hand through this process of trying to conceive and stay pregnant.

She told me I could conceive with a bicornuate uterus and that my hormone levels just needed to be worked out. She recommended that I take homeopathic supplements to start leveling hormones.

I felt invincible. My path was lit. I was ready to take supplements around the clock if need be.

Did God just answer my prayers? I could do this.

This path wasn't hopeless after all.

Lamentations 3:26 — "[I]t is good to wait quietly for the salvation of the LORD."

The midwife believed that the embryos weren't implanting properly; they weren't attaching to the uterine wall securely. "Supplements, progesterone, and plenty of rest would fix that," she said.

I was on cloud nine! The sky was a little bluer that day, and the birds sang a little louder. Craig and I were full of hope. We found the answer!

Acts 2:28 — "You have made known to me the paths of life; you will fill me with joy in your presence."

CHECKED OFF

Each month after that initial consultation with the midwife, we tried to conceive. Each month, we would be reminded just how much fertility was out of our hands. Our hope of the midwife having the answers was slowly fading away with each of those passing months.

The darkness of this path seemed unnavigable. Depression set in. The special diet. The supplements. Setting alarms as reminders for which pill to take next. The tracking of ovulation dates and so on felt daunting. The hope each month of getting a positive pregnancy test and then having that dream die was gut-wrenching. Trying to get pregnant was taking a toll.

The months were checked off the calendar one by one. Each month silently reminded us that a baby was not coming anytime soon. Craig confided in me that he started to feel like a sperm donor. He eventually asked me to stop telling him when I was ovulating.

"I don't understand your emotions," he said.

He believed we were going to have a baby, so the

fact that I was losing hope was foreign to him. I didn't feel encouraged by his solid belief. To the contrary, I felt alone. *Unseen.*

I didn't know where to turn or what to do. I prayed and read the Psalms constantly, finding momentary solace in King David's words.

My journal entries were few and far between. Many people write to process. I only wrote when I was happy. The silence of my pen was deafening. When I did write from a place of trying to process what was going on inside of me, my pages looked like child scribble. "Why?" was a constant question.

Why do we have to struggle? Why do we have to live in a broken world? Why? Why? Why?

Deuteronomy 32:10 — "In a desert land he found him, in a barren and howling waste. He shielded him and cared for him; he guarded him as the apple of his eye."

I never really got an answer from God when asking Him why we had to wait. But I did get His peace. In the dark moments of the night, lying in bed with my heart full of anguish, I would sense His presence. A new intimacy with the Lord was blossoming. It was like He was letting me ask—even challenge Him—about why getting pregnant was so hard. I wasn't in trouble for asking why. I was beckoned forth to share my heart with Him.

During this time of trying to conceive, the

unsolicited, cliché advice, "Stop trying to get pregnant and you'll get pregnant," came from the older church ladies.

It is awful advice. It implies that we can control our circumstances by pretending we aren't controlling them. I found that women love to give advice, and this was a constant piece of advice given to me.

I took their advice, sort of. I tried to stop trying for a baby. I gave up the calendar. Still, I couldn't stop hoping for my arms to be full. I was standing on God's promise, even if it was with shaky legs. The truth is, Craig and I never really stopped trying, even though we tried to tell ourselves otherwise.

I kept taking the supplements and did everything else the midwife told us to do.

It somehow seemed easier to act like I didn't care when someone would ask how things were going. I was beginning to build walls around my heart with other people. I didn't want the advice anymore.

I was no longer resting or sitting in my rocking chair, my place of remembrance of God's faithfulness. I would glance at it, but I dared not sit in it. Grieving each month without hope was death. I felt like I was dying.

I wanted to get my mind off waiting for a positive pregnancy test. I dove into work and college classes, working 60+ hours a week, taking on extra work assignments, and maintaining straight A's in my courses. These diversions were a way to no longer think about what I could not control.

I was becoming a workaholic. I loved it. I had closed off a part of my heart. I didn't want to hurt anymore. The only way I knew how to do that was to make my calendar full of activities.

I could control how much I worked. How much effort I put into my college essays. How much I volunteered at church. All ways to numb my heart, because the one thing I wanted most was the one thing I couldn't have.

I thought that if I could busy myself to the point where I would stop thinking about my empty arms, then I'd be fine. I tried to make myself feel better by ignoring my pain. Such a false sense of control. Such an unhealthy way to live.

It appeared that the cost of hope was too high. My good friend, Leticia, wrote to me:

> A toll is a price paid for our journey. Although Christ paid the ultimate price, our ransom, this life in Christ, in a fallen world, comes at a steep price.
>
> His promises are our hope. When what you are hoping for has yet to be realized, how can we use Scripture to seize hope? Is it possible to perceive pain and disappointment as earnest money for something greater to come?

Her question resonated deep within me. My hope for something greater was not gone, it was only hidden.

WAITING FOR HOME

A baby wasn't happening within my timeframe, but another miracle was brewing. I desperately wanted to move closer to my work, so we started looking for a new place.

Every apartment we loved was rented out before we brought back our rental application. Only a few weeks into our search, I was willing to settle for any old apartment. Craig was willing to wait for something spectacular.

Our options were few and far between with those kinds of prospects. I was beyond frustrated. However, Craig was peaceful in waiting, a mirror of our battle with infertility. He was at peace. I was not. Not only could I not control our fertility, but I could not control our housing situation, either.

As a young married couple, Craig and I were learning each other. I was learning that Craig's way of coping with loss, uncertainty, and uncontrollable circumstances was not inferior to mine. His quiet strength and patience in waiting were not how I wanted our lives to be handled, though.

Craig patiently waits to make decisions, weighing all the pros and cons while quietly trusting and praying. To the contrary, I rant, rave, and scream at God or anyone else within earshot. On a good day, our personality traits balance each other out.

I tend to jump in headfirst, then ask how deep the water is. He, on the other hand, sticks a toe in the water, calculating the temperature while drying off his foot.

I had to learn that waiting was not the opposite of persevering, but a complement to tenacity.

We discovered that many apartment buildings in the valley have permanent "For Rent" signs on their buildings when there wasn't vacancy. The turnover rate was so high that for efficiency's sake, the signs stayed up. If we wanted a place, we needed to move quickly.

I was working as an American Sign Language (ASL) interpreter for a high school in a suburban area with a beautiful park nearby. It reminded me of where I grew up in some nostalgic sort of way.

A cute, yellow, Spanish-style apartment was located across the street from the school. I noticed it a year earlier when there was a "For Rent" sign up for only a few days. I had not spotted another vacancy since then.

For some reason, I desperately wanted to live in that specific apartment. It was adorable.

Over the course of that year, I would park my car near that apartment and ask the Lord if we could live there, dreaming about what it would be like to just walk to work and not be stuck in LA traffic every day.

With no sign of a vacancy, it was a long shot. The weeks of looking at apartments with no options in our budget were exasperating. Finding a place that lived up to Craig's idea of spectacular was another miracle waiting to happen.

There was not even a hint of an answered prayer in the works. The illusion of control I loved so much was once again disappearing. My frustration level was at an all-time high.

A co-worker found a vacant apartment two miles from my workplace. She gave me the number. I left a voicemail with the landlord on Friday night asking about that apartment.

I gave my credentials for where I worked, pulling out all of the stops, trying to prove I was a good person, *aka* a good renter. Most LA landlords don't even call potential renters back. I was desperate.

Lo and behold, the landlord called back Saturday morning. For a brief moment, we had a misunderstanding.

"What?" I asked her over the phone. I was completely confused. "No, I wasn't calling about a yellow, Spanish-style building, I was calling about an apartment on another street."

"Well, you said you worked at the high school. I assumed you were calling about the yellow, Spanish-style apartment across the street from the school," the landlord replied.

My heart quickened. "Oh, wow! You own both buildings? I love that apartment!" came rolling off my tongue before I even realized the full meaning of what was happening.

"Wonderful! The apartment isn't for rent yet, but it will be in the next few days."

Her tenant had given a verbal move-out notice the night before. She needed a signed notice for it to be official.

What? How in the world does she own the building I called about last night AND the apartment I had been praying for? This is crazy!

Psalm 27:14 — "Wait for the LORD; be strong and take heart and wait for the LORD."

The wait had paid off. We made an appointment to see the apartment I had been dreaming about. Craig and I both loved it! It was the best place we had seen. It was our kind of spectacular.

We lovingly nicknamed our new apartment, "The Shoebox." It was all of 550 square feet, with a brand-new, one-butt kitchen. The next miracle: it was within our budget. We couldn't have been happier.

We ended up signing rental papers without there ever being an advertised "For Rent" sign up and without even knowing who to call about that building.

My faith was growing. We had an incredible answer to prayer and a crazy miracle to tell. We were beyond excited!

A PROMISE
ANNOUNCED

The promise of a baby still seemed so far away. Abraham and Sarah, even in their old age, had to wait 25 years for their promised baby. After staring at my rocking chair, I knew I needed to continue to hold onto the promise and not give up hope.

I sat in my modern-day altar, my place of remembrance, and cried out, "Dear God, please don't make me wait 25 years!"

I had met a woman who came to the agonizing decision to stop trying for children; a decision only she and her husband could make. A brave decision. I wasn't ready to make that choice yet. I really respected them for prayerfully coming to that conclusion. I also knew women who had spent thousands of dollars on fertility treatments with no results after years of waiting. My heart broke for them just as much as my heart was breaking for us.

It had been ten and a half months since Rachel had told me not to believe what those doctors said, and that God said I was going to have a baby. That promise might as well have been years old, because it felt that way.

Do God's promises expire?

One evening, I was pretty grumpy and feeling sick. Craig told me I was pregnant. "Go take a test," he said. I might as well have bought stock in pregnancy tests at that point. I wasn't going to spend another dime on a pregnancy test until I was at least a week late.

I told him, no, but then my curiosity got the best of me. I conceded.

He was right! We had a positive test! I screamed. I didn't believe it! So, I took another pregnancy test a few hours later.

Two positive pregnancy tests! What exciting news to receive shortly before Mother's Day!

Jeremiah 31:13b — "I will turn their mourning into gladness; I will give them comfort and joy instead of sorrow."

It was our fourth pregnancy in a little over three years. I was over the moon! Craig and I were both ecstatic.

That night, I wasn't apprehensive. I wasn't worried about miscarrying. It was as if all the months of praying and hoping had paid off. I was pregnant! I was ready to seize the promise. It was growing inside of me.

I called our midwife and was put on bedrest and progesterone immediately. I met with my boss to let her know I was leaving the school year early for bedrest.

We called our families. We called our friends.

One amazing couple, Foster and Michelle, our small group leaders at our little church, set up meals to be brought every other night for the next ten weeks to our home. They had been praying for us to conceive. We thanked them for their prayers and their kindness in organizing meals for us.

Craig and I were beyond excited! I was fully leaning into the joy of this pregnancy. This baby, our promised child, was on its way.

Bedrest, here I come!

Psalm 126:6 — "Those who go out weeping, carrying seed to sow, will return with songs of joy, carrying sheaves with them."

How to
Rest

During my first week of bedrest, I was full of adrenaline and hope because my long-awaited dream was happening. I was pregnant! But by the second week, reality set in.

Bedrest was not what I thought it was going to be. It was the worst prescription for a workaholic. It was stressful in a weird sort of way. I had gone from working crazy, long hours, trying to keep my mind off getting pregnant, to doing absolutely nothing. I was lying on the couch, watching movies, trying to stay pregnant.

I kept telling myself that for every minute I lay in bed or on the couch, it was another minute I was helping the placenta stay attached. I was working in my bedrest. I was working at keeping a growing baby in my uterus.

The morning sickness kicked in, but I wasn't vomiting as much as I had with our last pregnancy. I knew not to depend on that as a symptom anymore, like I had with the last baby. At some level, though, it was comforting to know my body knew I was pregnant.

I spent most of my days trying to be hopeful instead of anxious. But eventually, the uncertainty got the best of me.

What if we miscarry? I kept repeating in my mind. *What if bedrest doesn't fix anything? What if a bicornuate uterus is the right diagnosis? Then bedrest won't help anyway.*

The questions whirled around and around. I dove into Scripture and read books about waiting on the Lord. I prayed. I did everything I knew how to do to keep my mind from going crazy with the uncertainty of this pregnancy.

Hebrews 4:16 — "Let us then approach God's throne of grace with confidence, so that we may receive mercy and find grace to help us in our time of need."

I kept clinging to Scripture, hiding hope in my heart.

Romans 15:13 — "May the God of hope fill you with all joy and peace as you trust in him, so that you may overflow with hope by the power of the Holy Spirit."

This roller coaster was becoming a rather expected ride by now, but the emotions never felt routine. There were times I was peaceful, even joyful. Then I would panic. But I would come right back to peace and joy again.

Not knowing what was going on inside my body with this baby was agonizing. It made me want to have Superman's x-ray vision so I could see my promised baby growing. But in all practicality, I needed to walk by faith and not by sight.

> *1 Peter 5:7 — "Cast all your anxiety on him because he cares for you."*

I was learning to fight back uncertainty with hope. It was an action-oriented, spiritual sport. I kept repeating the scriptures about God's faithfulness.

> *Isaiah 40:31 — "[B]ut those who hope in the LORD will renew their strength. They will soar on wings like eagles; they will run and not grow weary, they will walk and not be faint."*

My midwife called with more bloodwork results. My pregnancy hormone levels looked to be in the low range, but not low enough to cause concern. She told us not to worry, we still had a viable pregnancy. We would do the bloodwork again in a couple days. I was coming to the end of my second full week of bedrest.

WHERE HEAVEN AND EARTH MEET

I never made it to the midwife for more bloodwork. On Saturday morning, I stood up from the couch slowly. I instantly started having sharp, stabbing pains in my lower abdomen. I walked to the bathroom. Blood and tissue gushed into the toilet.

My breath left me. My heart was seized by my chest. My hope died. I knew I was miscarrying. This was not spotting. It was labor. My uterus was contracting.

Tears poured down my face. I'd been through this before. I knew the routine.

Proverbs 13:12 — "Hope deferred makes the heart sick."

Praying under my breath, I called our midwife. She asked me to come in. I told her no because I knew this was a miscarriage. She advised me to come in anyway. The emotional pain of a miscarriage being confirmed at her office was too much for me to bear. I regretted calling her.

I knew there was nothing she could do to stop it. I knew roughly how much blood I could lose before I needed to go to the ER.

She asked me to stay in bed until Monday to see if the bleeding would stop. I knew it would lessen in a couple of hours or so. I had been down this road before.

I appeased her by saying that if I started hemorrhaging, I would go to the hospital.

Craig was at work. I called him. He offered to come home, but I thought I could handle it by myself. I would be fine, I thought. I told him to stay at work, pushing him away while still wanting him close. As soon as I hung up, I knew I wasn't going to be fine.

I called a friend from church to tell her that I was miscarrying. She happened to be headed to a baby shower for our mutual friend Bethany. I was excited for her because she was having a baby girl after experiencing loss herself. I was supposed to be there celebrating with her, but I was on bedrest. I found out later that a woman had asked that they pray for me at the shower—such a sweet gesture that meant the world to me.

Surprising myself, I realized I didn't actually want to be alone like I originally thought. I needed a friend close by who had faith in a God who seemed distant to me in that moment.

I called my friend, Meggan, who was moving out of state soon. She dropped everything, left her family, and drove the 45 minutes to my apartment. She ended up spending the day with me.

My face was red and puffy and my eyes swollen

and bloodshot by the time she arrived. My hope was gone. Almost a year of praying for a baby, and now, in just a few short weeks, this baby was gone. I was trying to cling to Jesus, but I realized I needed someone to be there while I did.

Meggan walked through my front door with her Bible and her arms full of food, the essential substances for our souls and bodies. A true burden-bearer. We sat on my living room couch together with our Bibles on our laps. She let me cry hot, ugly tears on her shoulder.

Her kindness in giving up her day will never be forgotten. She reminded me that God did love me. She said she would have hope for me to have a baby, even if I couldn't. She cried with me as she let me read the book of Psalms to her all day.

When my throat was too dry to read anymore, she took the Bible from my hands and continued to read where I left off. Peace washed over me the entire time with Meggan by my side. She was a physical reminder that Jesus was not far away, but sitting alongside me.

I had never experienced the scripture, "We mourn with those who mourn," as I did that day with Meggan. She didn't try to fix my pain with a how-to list. She just sat there with a heart full of compassion. We prayed the Psalms out loud for hours together. It was a holy moment.

> *Matthew 5:4 — "Blessed are those who mourn, for they will be comforted."*

Celtic Christians call these moments "The Thin Places" —the meeting points of Heaven and Earth. This was a thin place, a redemptive moment. I knew I wasn't alone. We were experiencing a touch of Heaven together.

BURDEN-BEARERS

Craig walked in from work that Saturday night. His jaw was set. His eyes were dark. I could tell he'd had a rough day. For the next 24 hours, we switched emotional roles.

I was full of peace that night, but he was distraught. I had never seen him like that before.

Lamentations 5:15 — "Joy is gone from our hearts; our dancing has turned to mourning."

Over the last year, he appeared to be the rock. He had all the peace. Now it was my turn to share my peace with him. After all, I had spent the day with Meggan in prayer, but he didn't have anyone to process with while at work.

My peace was not his peace, though. He was fuming with anger. It was the first time I saw him cry after one of our miscarriages. His anguish was in some way comforting to me. I didn't feel alone in my storm anymore. The previous miscarriages had been my burden alone to carry. Now, they were ours together.

Sunday morning came and went. We stayed home from church, following the midwife's orders. My peace from the night before was slowly fading away as the bleeding and sharp contractions continued into the afternoon.

I kept asking myself, *"How could a good God let this happen again?"*

We had waited almost a year for this baby to arrive. This baby, my baby, was here only for a few weeks. It seemed cruel. It seemed unlawful for God to give us hope and then take it away.

A friend called after church to tell us that one of the pastors, from the pulpit, had asked for prayer for us as we were going through another miscarriage. I was comforted, believing that people would pray.

An older woman in the church offered to bring us dinner. Craig was still angry. I was getting worried. His faith was rocked. He didn't want to be home when she came, so he went for a short walk.

She came in with homemade enchiladas. Unknowingly, she brought Craig's favorite dish. She sat down on the couch next to me. I whispered to her that he was angry with God. I was shaken by this admission. Could lightning strike us if we were that honest?

She said the most comforting words I will never forget: "That's okay. He's a big God, He can handle it."

My heart had been whirling for hours. Finally, in a single moment, it became still. "God already knows our thoughts, so let's be honest with sharing our hearts," was her sentiment.

That one phrase, "He's a big God, He can handle it," gave me permission to be real with myself and with Him. It gave me permission to say, "This stinks, God. I don't understand You."

Psalm 139:2 — "You know when I sit and when I rise; you perceive my thoughts from afar."

Our small group leaders, Michelle and Foster, called after dinner. I confessed to them that Craig was devastated and angry. I was scared by his visceral emotions.

Michelle asked, "Would he want to talk to Foster?"

"I don't know," I said, handing Craig the phone anyway.

Reluctantly, Craig put the phone to his ear and listened to Foster pray. I don't think he ever uttered a word. Witnessing my husband being cared for blessed me.

The beauty of that phone call wasn't in the words spoken. Just the opposite. It was all of the long, thoughtful pauses—not wanting to say something that would cause more devastation.

Foster and Michelle weren't in a hurry to hang up the phone. They were right there in our turbulent silence with us. The stillness was not uncomfortable; it was soothing. We were in the eye of the storm.

I'm pretty sure that between the woman dropping off his favorite meal and Foster praying for him, my husband's heart transformed from hardened coal to a semi-pulsating muscle. We were loved.

John 13:35 — "By this everyone will know that you are my disciples, if you love one another."

ONE SIMPLE QUESTION

On Monday, Craig and I drove to see the midwife. Bloodwork was done again.

How much blood can my body keep losing?

The results of my hormone levels showed that the baby only grew for a little over a week, but it took another week for my body to show the outward signs of a miscarriage.

She looked at my records in her lap, shaking her head. The confidence I saw in her months earlier was gone. Her shoulders were slumped over my chart. "Dammit, I'm so sorry, honey. I don't know why this keeps happening to you," she said with compassion. Her humanity brought comfort to my weary soul.

Thank you for cursing, Ms. Midwife. Thank you for saying something that I couldn't bring myself to say. Thank you for not being guarded with me. Thank you for not acting like you have all the answers. Thank you for looking at me as a person, as a woman, as someone with a broken heart, and not just as a patient or as a number in the computer, not as a dollar sign indicating how much money you can withdraw from our bank account. Thank you for being another woman who sees me for me.

Isaiah 66:12a,13a — "For this is what the LORD says: '...As a mother comforts her child, so will I comfort you...'"

"What's your blood type?" she asked.

"O negative," I replied.

"Okay, you'll need RhoGAM."

"What's that?"

"What? You don't know what RhoGAM is?" She was shocked. "Oh, honey, this could be why you keep miscarrying. No doctor has asked you what your blood type was before?"

"No!" I was still confused.

"If your blood and the baby's blood mix during the miscarriage and you don't get the RhoGAM shot, then your body could build antibodies in your blood to prevent any future pregnancies from progressing," she explained.

Anger rushed over my entire body. Medical negligence. How in the world, with all of the doctors I had seen—a different doctor with each miscarriage up until this point—did they *all* fail to ask me that one simple question?

I could be miscarrying because I didn't get a simple shot. Seriously?

Fire spread throughout my body. My anger took over my heart. I knew I needed a shot after the birth of a child, but it never occurred to me that I would need one after a miscarriage.

Why was that not on a doctor's checklist of questions? How could this be missed?

She gave me a referral to see a reproductive endocrinologist (RE), a doctor who specializes in infertility.

This is when I found out that not all OB-GYNs are created equal. Now, more than ever, we needed a specialist and a miracle. Our appointment was three weeks away. It seemed like an eternity.

My insides ached. The recognition that my childhood dream of growing up and having a family would not be coming true anytime soon.

My uterus ached. The contractions from a miscarriage are far worse than menstrual cycle cramps.

My head ached. The questions that went unspoken and unanswered festered. I was living out a long and torrid nightmare.

Forgetting that I was made in the image of God first and foremost, I continued to believe lies about myself. *If I'm not a mama, I'm not much of anything.* And, *If I don't have a working uterus, what good is it to be a woman?*

My trauma had a way of distorting the truth that I was made in the image of God, and it perpetuated the toxic false belief that my worth was only in what I could achieve or produce. My hope wasn't hidden. My hope was flushed down the toilet. My uterus was a graveyard for unborn children.

Job 7:11 — "Therefore I will not keep silent; I will speak out in the anguish of my spirit, I will complain in the bitterness of my soul."

I decided to turn to some older women in our little church who would have advice on infertility. With their wisdom, they could help me navigate the road ahead.

How to Numb the Light

One of the pastor's wives called and asked if I wanted to go with her to dinner. She had been mentoring me, but I had not seen her since my bedrest. After only four days since my confirmed miscarriage by the midwife, I jumped at the chance to get out of the apartment.

My heart had been shredded to pieces. It needed a surgeon with a careful hand to stitch it back together.

> *2 Samuel 22:7 — "In my distress I called to the LORD...he heard my voice; my cry came to his ears."*

We spotted a table on the patio and shuffled our chairs close to one another to settle in. As if I had just gotten back from a relaxing vacation, she asked, "How are you doing?"

I didn't pick up on her nonchalant, sanguine tone. "Well," I slowly confessed, "I feel like I'm in complete darkness. I don't understand why God would allow this to happen again."

My heart broke even more when I uttered the thoughts that had been whirling around my mind all week.

The pastor's wife's expression changed instantly. Her eyebrows knitted together. A frown spread across her lips. I couldn't understand her facial expression. My eyes searched hers for answers.

Suddenly, I recognized what I saw.

My heartbeat quickened. It was written all over her face. *Disapproval.*

My mind went blank. I sunk slightly in the chair. I felt a warm rush of shame wash over me.

She instructed me that I shouldn't be angry with God. This darkness I was feeling was evil. "You aren't processing this in a God-honoring way," she told me firmly, completely bypassing my emotions and misunderstanding my pain.

My heart reeled from the blow. My mind raced. I shouldn't have been so open, but she *was* mentoring me.

I thought I was supposed to tell the truth. Maybe I'm supposed to lie to make people feel comfortable. I feel disappointed and confused. Is that considered anger?

"Listen," she urged me. Her tone softened. "I think you're making an idol out of fertility." She paused. Reaching out to pat my hand, she said gently, "Maybe you are not supposed to have children. Let's not cry about this."

My heart turned stone-cold and sunk to the soles of my feet.

The pastor's wife just punched me in the gut. I felt ashamed for opening up my heart.

Her words seemed to contradict her own value system. At our little church, pregnant women and mothers were highlighted at women's ministry events, but not women who didn't have children. Fertility seemed to be highly valued among the church ladies. I had never heard it mentioned from the pulpit that a woman's worth was not in her motherhood.

Any last bit of hope I had been holding onto was gone. Hijacked. I slid my hand out from under hers— off the table, and into my lap.

The color drained from my face. I regretted talking. I regretted sharing my heart. My story.

If she misunderstood my deep desire for children as an idol, then she must have forgotten about the women of the Bible, like Sarah, Rebekah, Rachel, Manoah's wife, and Elizabeth, who all cried out to God for a miracle beyond human reasoning. But, the words wouldn't come out of my mouth.

I need to get home now.

Subconsciously obeying her words, the tears dried up, missing in action. I gulped down my emotions. I absorbed her admonishment.

Surprisingly, I wasn't angry with *her*. I became angry with *myself*.

I reasoned that she was right. After all, she had experienced miscarriages herself years before, all without shedding a tear. She made it sound like she never doubted God. I assumed she was a superhero for not crying over her own losses. If crying was wrong, I didn't want to cry.

Forgetting that God isn't a man who can lie, my mind spun like a merry-go-round that would never stop.

Maybe I am making an idol out of fertility. After all, the medical community labeled me as infertile. Maybe God did, too. She's right, I'm not made to have children.

Numbers 23:19 — "God is not human, that he should lie, not a human being, that he should change his mind. Does he speak and then not act? Does he promise and not fulfill?"

When dinner was over, we parted ways. I arrived home, internally waving my white flag. I was done hoping for a child, let alone children. God's promise had expired. I surrendered. I never told Craig about this conversation. I kept it hidden. I didn't want him to tell me she was right.

It never occurred to me that Craig or anyone else would tell me it wasn't I who was wrong, but the pastor's wife.

My trauma colored the world. I needed my Savior who died and rose again to make His presence known to me. So that I would no longer see the world through the lens of trauma, but through the lens of hope and healing through Jesus. I needed a careful surgeon, not a judge.

If she had recognized my loss as a death, maybe her advice wouldn't have been to ignore the darkness;

it would have been to grieve the loss of my children.

I'd suffered through four deaths of little lives gone too soon from my family. If she had acknowledged that darkness comes with suffering, she might have comforted me instead of telling me not to cry.

If she had attended funerals for each of my babies, maybe she would have understood that the darkness I was experiencing was that of extreme, complicated sorrow and ensuing complex trauma.

> *Psalm 116:3 — "The cords of death entangled me, the anguish of the grave came over me; I was overcome by distress and sorrow."*

Seven years after my meeting with the pastor's wife that day, I read a book on shame and vulnerability, called, *Daring Greatly,* by Dr. Brené Brown. The book imparted a powerful concept to me that changed my perspective about being honest in sharing my emotions. In the words of Brené Brown, "Owning our story can be hard but not nearly as difficult as spending our lives running from it [because] when you numb the darkness you numb the light."

I had spent seven years sinking in shame, judging myself for mourning uncontrollably and for sharing my story—supposedly wrong for trying to understand why I felt so lost. After reading Brené Brown's book, I could finally look back upon that fateful dinner outing with new eyes.

The pastor's wife, whom I had allowed to mentor

me, was more than twice my age. She had never given herself permission to mourn her own miscarriages. She had never given herself permission to be real with God, or with others. She had never allowed Jesus to shine His light to heal the pain of her darkness.

Her generation didn't talk about miscarriages and infertility. Here I was, unknowingly deviating from the social norm. She was only treating me the way she had treated herself.

My honesty triggered the brokenness she had never dealt with. My words had pried open her wounded heart.

She believed wrestling with God was not an option. I believed God was allowing me to wrestle with Him. I was following in the footsteps of Jacob, refusing to let go of God until He blessed me. "He's a big God, He can handle it," is still the best advice I have ever received when it comes to grief and loss.

TWO UNSPOKEN
FEARS

Later that evening, I was home alone, sitting in the dark, slumped over in my rocking chair in a catatonic state. I stared into the nothingness before me.

I had not been expecting that dinner conversation to go the way it did. The words of the pastor's wife were shrapnel to my already wounded soul. All night, I kept replaying the conversation in my mind, wishing I had explained myself better, but believing she was right.

My thoughts were incoherent and disconnected. A memory from my childhood flashed before me like an image on an old TV screen. I was playing outside with a little girl. We were four or five years old, playing "house." I played the mama, and the little girl played my daughter. The TV signal weakened, and the memory went fuzzy. Then blank.

That dream was not meant to be.

I was not a mother. As far as I was concerned, I was worthless.

Craig had been working late into the night. He came home and walked into our bedroom, where I was rocking. He flipped on the lights.

The bright lights triggered my numb body back to life for a moment. I didn't look at him. I stared into the abyss of our childless future. Thoughts were absent.

"Are you okay?" he asked.

His words didn't register.

Louder, he said, "Hey, Babe. You okay?"

I looked up from the rocking chair and quietly said, "I want a divorce."

"What?! Why?"

Calmly, coldly, I repeated, "I want a divorce."

"Why?" he pleaded. "Why?" he begged. He knelt down by the rocking chair. "What happened to you? Where is this coming from?"

I didn't tell him about my earlier conversation with the pastor's wife.

Becoming more hysterical with each word, I began to explain, "I am not made to have children. You will be a great dad, and I can't give you children!" My words ended in a screaming shrill.

My words stung him. They stung my own heart. No tears came to my eyes. It was as if a desert had taken over my mind, my body, and my soul.

"You're being ridiculous! I'm not divorcing you," he said with heated breath.

He turned to walk away.

"Why not?" I screamed. "You deserve better than me! You deserve a woman who can give you children!"

He abruptly walked out of the room as if the conversation was out of the question.

My anger boiled over. How dare he leave! I ran after him, yelling, "See, you're going to walk away from me when you figure out I'm defective." My voice broke. "You're going to leave me! Why can't you realize I'm broken?!" I screeched.

Tears streamed down my face as I continued, "I'm used up. I'm not a woman! I'm no good! Divorce me! I dare you!" I fell into a heap on the floor of our living room, sobbing uncontrollably with my face buried in the carpet.

My husband turned around to face me and grunted, "No, I am not leaving you!" But then his anger melted. He knelt on the floor next to my fractured soul. He said firmly, yet compassionately, "I'm staying right here."

Craig moved towards me with tears welling up in his eyes. I pulled away. "Don't touch me!" I warned. "You don't understand!" I choked out the words, not looking at him.

Unarticulated thoughts ran through my mind.

If I'm single, then people will stop asking me if I'm pregnant. They'll stop asking if we're going to have kids. I need to be single. If I'm single, the pain will stop.

I now lay as though lifeless on the floor.

Craig moved from kneeling to lying next to my limp body. I was defeated. With great hesitation, he reached for my hand. I reluctantly let him hold my hand in his. He fiddled with my wedding band on my finger, slowly spinning it.

We both lay there in silence, staring at the ceiling. At first under his breath, and then louder, he started praying for me. With each sentence spoken, a holy confidence took over his voice. "God, we don't get it. We don't understand why we keep miscarrying. But we pray for peace."

I didn't want him to pray for me. I'd had enough of prayer. But I didn't stop him. As he continued to pray, my heart softened. My body and soul slowly revived. He prayed well into the night. An unexplainable peace came over me. God was there in my darkest hour. In my ugliness, in my despair. God was there.

For the first time that night, I spoke my fears, rooted in trauma, rooted in the pit of Hell, out loud to my husband. "If I am barren, you will leave me. If I can't have children, then I am of no value to our marriage."

Psalm 139:8 — "If I go up to the heavens, you are there; if I make my bed in the depths, you are there."

WHEN NO ONE ELSE KNOWS

The next few weeks were a blur of sleepless nights and groggy days. Little did I know that insomnia is a huge symptom of depression. I laid awake at night, not wanting to pray.

Regardless, I found myself praying under my breath as my husband slept soundly next to me.

What are you thinking, God? People keep telling me that this baby must not have been in Your timing. Is that true? Do you kill children if the timing isn't right? That doesn't make any sense!

Psalm 73:21-22 — "When my heart was grieved and my spirit embittered, I was senseless and ignorant; I was a brute beast before you."

The questions were like water in a storm drain in the middle of a downpour. I counted the seconds until dawn, wondering what life would hold for me that day.

Before the dawn arrived, in the middle of the blackened night, a cacophony of voices shouted opinions at me. Advice from well-meaning friends. Advice from the church ladies. Advice from earlier conversations, during which all I could manage was a plastered smile.

"Just adopt," the voices said. *"Maybe God has other plans for you. You should be content,"* and so on. I couldn't get the voices out of my head.

I just wanted to scream, "Shut up! Shut up! Shut up!" But those voices of well-meaning friends and family felt firmly planted in my head now. If I held my head with my hands pressed against my ears, in the silence of the night, would the voices stop tormenting me? My mental health was deteriorating from the trauma of losing my babies and the pain of feeling all alone.

I couldn't stop replaying the awful conversations in my mind. The tape recorder's repeat button had been turned on, and I couldn't find the off switch.

Hannah, I thought. *Why can't I be like Hannah?* She mourned with such abandonment that the priest thought she was drunk.

Could I wail like that? Obviously not in front of anyone—that's unacceptable in our Western culture. But I desperately wanted to wail. I needed to wail.

Instead, I held back my emotions. I laid in bed staring at the ceiling. There was no visible emotion. No tears. A cloud of darkness hovered over me.

The depression, the hopelessness, the pain, the numbness, and the tragedy of my story of motherhood ending in yet another loss were too much to bear. I forgot about the kindness shown to me by good friends weeks earlier.

Forgetting that God is near the broken-hearted, the darkness became too great. Life was not worth living. My plans for a baby had failed. My husband refused to leave me, but I didn't trust his words to be true. *He could change his mind any minute,* I thought.

I laid next to him, watching him as he slept soundly.

How could he go from peace about having children to being angry at God and back to peace so quickly after this miscarriage?

I was jealous of his resolved faith.

I slowly got up from bed, removing the covers ever so carefully as not to disturb him. I tiptoed to our bathroom's medicine cabinet and searched through the bottles: Advil. NyQuil. Pepto Bismol.

Dammit, nothing strong enough to knock me out, only enough pills to have some doctor pump my stomach.

Even my haphazard plans to OD were failing. I slid to the floor with my back against the wall. *Defeated.*

Does the agony ever stop?

A stifled groan escaped from me. No words from my mouth came, just the deep, raw pain of unspeakable sorrow.

There on the bathroom floor, a faint song found its way into my heart:

You lift me up and help me stand,
You run to me with outstretched hands.

I wasn't running to God in my darkness—He was running to me. He ran to me like a father who hears his child's cry.

Romans 8:26 — "In the same way, the Spirit helps us in our weakness. We do not know what we ought to pray for, but the Spirit himself intercedes for us through wordless groans."

The song washed over me. My spirit cried out, almost as if it were a passive bystander, when I had nothing left to give.

My spirit uttered a song I had sung countless times over the last twelve months:

You run to me with outstretched hands.

There God was, wrapping His arms around me again, even when I thought I didn't deserve it.

His grace covered me even still. Unearned, unmerited, and undeserved forgiveness, love, and mercy were freely given to me in my deepest pain. He was giving me a new tape recorder to play in my head: *He loves me enough to run to me, just as I am.*

A Mama's
Prayer

My desperation to numb the pain and stop the agony turned into a surrender of sorts, but not a holy surrender of "God, your will be done."

It was the kind of surrender that says, "If trying for a family costs this much, I don't want a family." It was the kind of surrender that says, "It costs too much to hope, to pray, and to believe in an unseen miracle."

There were no words to express this surrender. I told Craig I was done—done with dreaming, done with planning the layout of a nursery, done with thinking of paint colors for nursery walls. Done. Stick-a-fork-in-me done.

He wasn't willing to throw in the towel just yet, but he gave in to avoid another outburst from his wife.

Psalm 38:6 — "I am bowed down and brought very low; all the day long I go about mourning."

I made a phone call to my parents. I told my mama

that we were done trying. I didn't tell her about the dinner conversation with the pastor's wife and how it almost killed me. I didn't tell her about my screaming for a divorce. I didn't tell her about my toying with the idea of suicide.

I was learning to compartmentalize the pain. I didn't know how to process the despair of losing another child.

I just wanted out of the hell hole of infertility. So, I told my mama I was just empty. Deep down I knew my value was not in what my womb could produce, but in the identity of Christ. Yet I was blinded by the pain and could not see that truth clearly.

I told her I was going to cancel the appointment with the RE. Our insurance would only cover a small percentage of the visit anyway. We would have to dip into our savings for that visit and any future visits. I wasn't sure if it was wise to spend more money than we already had with no guaranteed outcome.

I didn't want to lay on another exam table with my bare feet in cold stirrups. I didn't want to fill out more medical forms. I didn't want to fight with the insurance company. I didn't want to hope. I didn't want to feel anything. My heart felt too heavy to even beat.

I was a walking, breathing shell of a person. I had heard stories of military personnel coming back from combat, and in some weird way, I could relate. Once you have experienced death and destruction, you can't comprehend how life—a truly fulfilling life—could ever be attained again.

On the phone, my mom asked me to keep my

doctor's appointment; at least to see if we could get answers as to why we kept miscarrying. I conceded to keeping the appointment just for her.

She reminded me that she would believe for a baby for us. She wasn't going to give up hope. She would keep praying. I admired her determination. She was strong and stubborn. She wouldn't take "no" for an answer.

"Okay, Mom. *You* can pray for a baby, but not me."

"That's fine, Linni. God has big plans for you. You're just too hurt to see them yet," she replied.

My mom asked me to fly home so she could hold me. Having MS, she couldn't do much, but she could console me. Here she was again, being my biggest cheerleader. My parents bought a plane ticket for me to fly home to Ohio in seven weeks. All I had to do was hold on for seven more weeks. I could do that.

"Okay, Mama, I'll go to the doctor. I'll see what he says. If you want me to keep praying, I will." I conceded once more.

I found myself rolling my eyes at this ludicrous idea as if I were a teenager again.

I'll keep hoping against all earthly odds for a miracle baby, Mama, just for you.

A HOLY
STUBBORNNESS

Shortly after my conversation with my mama, I awoke from a deep sleep in such terror that my heart raced. My body was covered in a cold sweat. In the darkness, a miracle story flooded my mind; the story of how I was born, and survived.

The story has become a part of my DNA. I was born ten weeks before my due date, a preemie. Apparently, a sizable one at that. I was born 3 lbs., 10 oz. in the middle of a blizzard in the early 1980's. Against all the odds the doctors gave my parents, I survived the night.

After surviving the first night, I wasn't expected to live the rest of the week. The story my parents tell is that my father went into his office at work, shut the door, and planned my funeral. My mother didn't visit me in the NICU that first week.

She couldn't bear the idea of her baby dying. When I survived the first night and then the next and the next, the doctors and nurses nicknamed me, "The Fighter."

God was reminding me that I was a fighter. I am a fighter—a stubborn fighter. It is both my greatest strength and my greatest weakness. It is both my superpower and my kryptonite.

My dad often said, sometimes out of complete exasperation over my stubbornness, sometimes out of awe of my tenacious spirit, "Linni, God knew what He was doing when He made you so stubborn." My dad believed it was the reason I survived.

My dad reminded me of the story of my birth throughout my growing-up years, of God's hand in my life from the very first breath I ever took. The story rattled in my mind as I bolted awake in the wee hours of the morning. I suddenly realized how much I had limited God in my throwing in the towel. I had stopped fighting for a victory.

There was no scolding voice from above—no tinge of guilt in my heart—just a holy, awe-filled moment with God. The kind that says, "You made the universe, and I am only a small part of this universe." An awe that says, "You are God, and I am not." An awe that makes one shake in one's boots before a powerful king. An awe mixed with terror that says, "I've made a mistake. I will not pretend to play God in my own life. I will fight if You tell me to fight."

The fear that I had limited God's hand was so palpable, I could taste it. The fear and awe that He knows what He's doing, and I do not. The fear and the joy mixed into one at the realization that the pain of my babies being gone was not the end of my story, but possibly the beginning. He was telling me to fight this battle.

For me, in this moment, a holy surrender was saying, *"Okay, God, if you want me to have faith that*

I'm going to have a baby, then I'll keep on believing and hoping against all odds. I'll cling to hope. I'll hide it in my heart. I won't let go of your promise."

My hope revived. My mama's prayers were heard.

---

2 Corinthians 5:7 — "For we live by faith, not by sight."

This was the kind of surrender God wanted from me: "Not my will be done, but Yours." My will said, "I don't want to hurt anymore," but His will said, "Let me write a better story."

Where I put a period, He put a comma. Where I wrote, "The End," He wrote, "In the beginning."

I was gaining a holy stubbornness. He was writing my story. This was just the beginning. I was learning to hold onto 2 Corinthians 5:7, "For we live by faith, not by sight."

AN OPEN
DOOR

The day finally arrived for us to knock on yet another door, to meet the RE. It seemed like it was years ago that we made the appointment at the midwife's office, but in all reality, it had only been three weeks.

Matthew 7:7 — "Ask, and it will be given to you; seek, and you will find; knock, and it will be opened to you."

Sorrow made me feel like I had aged beyond my years, like life had sped by. Hope and anticipation, by contrast, made me feel as if time had stopped. The appointment made a few weeks earlier seemed to have been made before I was born. Time couldn't move fast enough for this day to arrive. How the emotions of sorrow and hope can happen at the same time, I will never know.

If the midwife's office could have had an antithesis, it would be this office. We opened the door to the most gorgeous lobby I had ever seen. We just walked into what looked like a million-dollar office.

Muted green walls, gray marble coffee tables, and modern, clean lines of black leather couches and chairs decorated the room. The ceiling lights were not ordinary lights, but gorgeous tiered crystal chandeliers. The lobby featured a beautiful stone waterfall fountain. A smoky glass wall separated the lobby from the back offices.

Greenery was placed meticulously throughout the office. A large flat screen TV with mahogany framing was mounted on the main wall. A coffee and tea station was set up in the corner.

We had just opened the door to the most posh medical office I had ever seen.

Oh, this appointment is going to be expensive! Hello, and welcome to Hollywood.

A nurse took us back to the doctor's office, where the doctor was waiting at his desk. We sat across from him. I spotted my medical chart open on his desk. My medical history from three different doctors and the midwife was all in one place. Just the facts. None of the turmoil, none of the trauma my heart and soul had been through, none of the desperation to find answers. Just the facts, including that I'd had four miscarriages in three years and was all of 24 years old.

Would he see me, or would I be another faceless patient on his schedule?

He shook hands with us and got right to his point. "I'm so sorry to see how much heartache you've been through."

Hallelujah! I knew we found the right doctor for us! I thought. I breathed a sigh of relief. *He sees me. He sees us.*

"I'm looking through both your medical charts and Craig's semen analysis. His sperm count is high, and his motility is healthy. So that doesn't seem to be the issue. But I believe that your bicornuate uterus diagnosis is wrong. Looking at these past ultrasounds, it looks more like you have a septum in your uterus. I want to do bloodwork to make sure we're not dealing with anything else."

I was immediately impressed with his approach— a let's-fight-this-head-on kind of attitude. He was direct and willing to work with us. My hope was alive and active. I was ready to do anything he said. If he said jump, I would say, "How high?" I was sold. This was our doctor.

"Let's do an ultrasound right now to see what I can find today," he said.

He led us to an exam room. A few minutes later, my lap was draped with a pink medical blanket, and my bare feet were placed in stirrups, the most awkward position there ever could be. I lost count of how many times I had been in this position over the last couple of years, but it was getting to be ridiculous.

The doctor's eyes scanned the ultrasound screen. He pointed to a blackened-gray area. "Do you see this?" he asked.

"Yes," I said, not really seeing a difference between where he was pointing and the rest of the gray and black screen, but I desperately wanted to see the answers he seemed to see.

"You do have a septum. I won't know the extent of it until we do a hysterosalpingogram."

"What's that?"

"A hysterosalpingogram, or HSG for short, is similar to an x-ray taken of your uterus, fallopian tubes, and ovaries with dye that's injected to see if there are any abnormalities in your reproductive organs," he explained.

I asked, "How soon can we do the procedure?"

He responded nonchalantly with a shrug of his shoulders, "Early next week."

I was overjoyed that answers were right around the corner. I felt like I'd just walked through the largest open door ever!

In another room, a nurse drew vials of blood from my arm—more than any other medical professional had drawn in my entire life combined—to be sent off to their express lab. We would have results the next morning for any abnormal hormone levels.

Craig left the office with a spring in his step. I, however, left the office a bit woozy from all the blood drawn. But if a heart could skip with joy, mine did that day. The doctor was hopeful, and we were even *more* hopeful. He breathed new hope into us.

THE FLOODGATES OPENED

The following week, we were back at the RE's office. We found out that my hormone levels were normal, so the only visible issue for miscarrying was having a septum.

This HSG procedure would determine if the septum could be removed. We ended up liquidating some stocks in our investment portfolio to pay for it, since our insurance wouldn't cover what they called "an elective procedure."

The doctor gave me a prescription for Valium so I would stay calm during the procedure. I was anxious about being given any drug because of how I had reacted adversely to so many other medications in the past.

I told myself that if he was giving me Valium, it must be needed. But it backfired! I wasn't calm at all! So instead of being calm during the pre-procedure, I ended up in a cold sweat the entire time!

"You're seriously not going to stick all of those instruments in me, are you?" I asked in a panic. Three large wands were on a small table next to the ultrasound machine.

"Yes, that's how it's done," the doctor chuckled, amused at my question.

Oh my god! I should have asked more questions before we started.

"Oh, dear God!" I vented. I took a deep breath, wishing I had been put under anesthesia instead of having to stay conscious during this part.

"It shouldn't hurt," he said, trying to reassure me. *Yeah, right.*

Craig held my hand. The lights were turned off, and just the glow of the ultrasound screen illuminated the room.

The doctor injected the dye into my uterus. He moved around, trying to get a better angle, but he couldn't see anything.

"The dye isn't going in."

"Yeah, I know, I can feel it burning," I said as the dye was running out on the exam table.

"It shouldn't be burning you," he muttered.

"Well, it is," I said calmly, trying to hold back tears.

"Okay, I'm going to inject more dye."

I held my breath. "Okay." I squeezed my husband's hand.

A few agonizing minutes later, the doctor said, "It isn't working. I don't know why the dye isn't staying in." He was perplexed.

We just wasted thousands of dollars. All of my hope had been put into finding answers that day.

The dam broke. I hadn't cried since I told Craig I wanted a divorce weeks earlier, but when the doctor told me it wasn't working, all of the unshed tears that had been simmering just poured out of my eyes, right there with the dye on the exam table.

The waterworks wouldn't stop. We hit another dead end. Another door closed in our faces. My hopes were dashed yet again, this time against the most jagged of rocks. I had stuffed all my tears away, but now they were coming and couldn't be held back.

"Please, please try again." I begged, trying ineffectively to hold back the floodgates.

"Are you okay? This really shouldn't hurt that badly."

The dye burning, the ache of having empty arms, the weight of grieving—all of it was too much to bear. It all compounded in that moment on that exam table.

"I'm fine, I think the Valium is making me emotional," I said, wiping away tears, embarrassed that I couldn't hold it together in the exam room. But the hot tears just kept streaming down my face.

If tears get stuffed down in the quiet of a private place, they have a way of escaping in the most public of places.

So, there I was, with tears streaming down my face and into my ear canals. If hope was a balloon, it was being deflated in front of me. Within fifteen minutes of starting the procedure to the doctor leaving the room shaking his head and wondering why it didn't work, my hope went from soaring high to crashing to the ground and burning.

The doctor suggested we do the procedure again, but with an anesthesiologist at his Malibu office.

Why didn't we do that in the first place?

We agreed to do the procedure again, even though we didn't have any guarantees that the second procedure would work either.

My stubbornness was kicking in. In the midst of my tears, suddenly my hope came back to life. Determination set in.

We'll keep fighting. Let's do it! We'll go to Malibu!

We sold more investment stocks. We were desperate to find answers. I didn't learn until years later that desperation is another part of grief.

Let's knock on another closed door.

Psalm 119:50 — "My comfort in my suffering is this: Your promise preserves my life."

THREE TRUTHS FOR
EVERY ONE LIE

After the HSG procedure didn't work, inadequacy filled my thoughts. I had peace about doing the HSG. But it didn't reveal what I hoped it would. My uterus not only couldn't hold children, but it also couldn't hold liquid dye.

What's wrong with me?

The RE explained that while I was in utero, at only eight weeks of gestation, my septum was formed. I was a miracle baby with a birth defect, an invisible imperfection.

I had been broken my entire life and oblivious to it.

Geez. Then why give me the desire to have children, God?

It seemed cruel.

My wrestling with questions, with God, and with myself were all compiled into believing that God's sovereign plan needed some fixin'. My own feeling of inadequacy made me believe that God Himself had inadequate plans for my life.

Proverbs 19:21 — "Many are the plans in a person's heart, but it is the Lord's purpose that prevails."

My friend Bethany called me. She told me she couldn't wait for me to come over and hold her newborn baby girl.

Her words didn't quite register.

Wait, was she asking me to hold her baby? What was she thinking? I kill everything I touch: plants, flowers, and babies.

I realized at that point that I didn't trust myself enough to even touch another person's child. I thought that if my uterus could kill four babies, then my touch could, too. What a ludicrous idea! But in my sorrow, ludicrous ideas ran rampant and showed up in the ugliest of ways.

Lies beget more lies. I blamed myself for my babies being gone. I was an incompetent mother whose own children didn't want to be in her arms. The lies were easy to believe. The truth always comes out, though, even if it takes years to be revealed.

She doesn't think I'll harm her newborn?

She trusted me to hold her baby girl. I will never be able to hold the baby I just lost, but I could love on someone else's miracle baby.

Here was Bethany, graciously knowing my desire to have a baby. She acknowledged my longing for children. Her compassion toward me solidified our friendship. We could talk about pain and loss *and* her children and cooking and art and life.

Somehow, having a conversation about her children didn't feel like it was being shoved in my face like it did with other women. I was being welcomed into her life, because we didn't just talk about parenthood, but about a million other things, too. She made me believe that just being me, without a baby in my arms, was enough for a friendship; that my value as a woman wasn't placed in fertility. She held space for me in the uncertain journey of infertility.

Lamentations 3:22-24 — "Because of the LORD's great love we are not consumed, for his compassions never fail. They are new every morning; great is your faithfulness. I say to myself, 'The LORD is my portion; therefore I will wait for him.'"

JESUS AND
VALIUM

The night before the second HSG procedure, I was so anxious that I gave myself a panic attack. Since the first procedure failed, we had been warned of too many possible outcomes, too many errors that could happen, and too many mistakes that could be made.

Right then and there, I knew I had to make a choice: either trust God, or stay in anxiety-ridden mode about the following morning's procedure.

> *Isaiah 12:2 — "Surely God is my salvation; I will trust and not be afraid. The LORD, the LORD himself, is my strength and my defense; he has become my salvation."*

The odds were not in our favor. This was our last hope. The RE had already explained that if the second HSG didn't work, there was nothing else we could do. Infertility would be our fate.

That night, Craig and I made a choice. Our choice

and our prayer was, "Your will be done, not ours, Lord." It's a simple prayer to say, but it's a difficult prayer to believe. When I exhaled this prayer out of the depths of my soul and into the air as a whisper lifted on high, peace flooded my mind.

A lot was riding on this test. In my heart, no matter the outcome, I chose to believe we were in God's hands. Our church prayed. Friends prayed. Family prayed. We prayed. It gave me something to do with my mind when anxious thoughts were threatening my every waking moment.

The following morning, we entered the doctor's office with the peace that only the Holy Spirit could bring. I calmly waited in the lobby. I calmly waited through the setup with the anesthesiologist. I calmly waited for the procedure to start.

Craig and I were both surprised at our even-keeled manner. Jesus was in the room.

Prayer calmed my thoughts. Prayer relieved the panic. Prayer lowered my heart rate.

I woke up from the procedure not knowing if it had worked. The doctor waited for Craig to come in. He couldn't hide the smile on his face. I held my breath, waiting for his words to match his grin. The procedure was a success! Our prayers had been answered!

Isaiah 26:4 — "Trust in the LORD forever, for the LORD, the LORD himself, is the Rock eternal."

The RE confirmed with 100% confidence that I had

miscarried because of the septum. It was so large that it couldn't be removed all at once. We would have to schedule two surgeries for the following month.

We were told that once the surgeries were over, we would be able to start trying again in six to eight weeks! It was the best news we had heard in a long time! We were one step closer to our dream of raising the next generation!

No Tears
Allowed

One Sunday morning at our little church, right before the sermon was about to start, I slipped out of the sanctuary and towards the bathroom. As I pushed the bathroom door open, I heard a stifled cry and stopped in my tracks.

I didn't know who was hidden in the stall. I shut the door behind me so no one else could hear the whimpering. I whispered, "Hey, it's Linni. Are you okay?"

The door to the stall flung open. "Oh, Linni, I'm so glad it's you!" she sobbed as she threw her arms around me. Not quite knowing what she meant by that, I just hugged her back.

"What's wrong?" I asked.

"I'm miscarrying," she said with tears as she pulled away to look me in the eyes.

My face dropped. My heart sank to the pit of my stomach. Tears filled my eyes, matching hers. "Oh, I'm so sorry."

"We went for our ultrasound on Friday, but they couldn't find a heartbeat."

"I'm so sorry." My heart knew this pain all too well. I didn't have any other words to say.

"I started bleeding this morning. I don't want anyone to see me cry." Embarrassed, she quickly wiped away her tears, trying to compose herself.

Psalm 6:6 — "I am worn out from my groaning. All night long I flood my bed with weeping and drench my couch with tears."

I knew what she meant when she wiped away her tears. It seemed tears were seen as, "you don't trust God."

I asked if I could pray for her. I knew there weren't any words that could bring comfort. I knew no prayer spoken out of my own humanness would bring clarity to all of her unspoken whys. I only knew to ask Jesus to wrap His arms around her.

I felt helpless as I witnessed her tears and brokenness. It was a visible mirror to my own pain.

Sitting in the service a few minutes later, I couldn't shake the words she had spoken to me: "I don't want anyone to see me cry."

It was one thing to keep my own emotions close to my heart, but to realize that someone *else* was wearing a mask too, not wanting people to see *her* broken heart, was a different story. Every fiber of my being felt hot with fiery anger.

How many of us stand in front of the mirror every morning, hoping to paint a beautiful picture that hides our brokenness?

> *Psalm 56:8 — "Record my misery; list my tears on your scroll—are they not in your record?"*

The emotional exposure seemed too great for both of us.

SPEED BUMPS VS. ROADBLOCKS

The first surgery to remove part of the septum was scheduled for six weeks after my HSG test. But two weeks later, the surgeon's office called to let us know they had a cancellation. All of my pre-op appointments were moved up. We only had one week to get everything in order.

I was a basket case of nerves. Prior to the operation, my blood needed to be drawn in case there was hemorrhaging, paperwork needed to be filled out to petition the insurance company to cover the surgery, and I needed a vacation from reading all the warnings on the medical release forms!

A high probability that I could wake up with a punctured uterus or perforated intestines did nothing to help my anxiety level.

"That's no big deal," the doctor said. "If it happens, we'll just give you medication to seal everything back up."

Great, just what I wanted to hear.

Two days prior to the operation, the insurance company was still saying they wouldn't cover an elective cosmetic surgery, let alone two surgeries. We couldn't believe their reasoning! It wasn't like I was asking for a tummy tuck.

Yet again, we were at the mercy of God. I believed this was the direction we needed to go, but we slammed right into another dead end.

My hope was on the line. I wanted to go ahead with the surgeries even though we would have to pay out of pocket. Craig wanted to wait and see what all of our options were.

I took Craig's approach as saying, "I'm having cold feet about having children," which wasn't at all what he meant, but I desperately wanted to do anything we could do to fix my body. I wanted to jump in headfirst, and he wanted to test the water. I was beyond frustrated with him. We both decided to pray separately about what we were supposed to do.

I felt strongly that we were being asked to be like the Levite priests and walk into the Jordan River. God told them to walk forward, even though they were walking into a flowing river. We needed to get wet. Our ankles needed to be soaked before God would part the river for us.

But I held my tongue. I really wanted us to be on the same page, but I didn't want to influence his process of seeking and reflecting with the Lord.

Psalm 46:10a — ..."Be still, and know that I am God..."

That evening, Craig told me he believed we were

supposed to go ahead with the operation. I was both relieved and elated that I didn't have to yell and scream to get my way. We were on the same page. "Let's do whatever it takes," he said.

The outpatient surgical center wanted a payment plan established before the surgery. We decided to call in the morning to get things set up.

The next morning, the day before the first surgery, the surgeon's office beat us to the punch. They called to let us know the negotiations with the insurance company were successful. It took three times of faxing them paperwork, which explained in detail the necessity for the outpatient surgery, for them to agree to cover 80% of the cost.

This was our parting of the Jordan River. In a matter of hours, we went from 0% coverage to 80% coverage.

I was learning that what I saw as roadblocks, God only saw as speed bumps. I wasn't being stopped in my tracks. I was just being asked to slow down. Kneel. Pray. Seek. Let miracles happen. I was learning to say, "Thank you, God, for speed bumps."

Vacuums, Prayers, and Miracles!

The day of surgery arrived. While I was lying on the hospital bed waiting to be wheeled into the OR, my nurse kept repeating the phrase, "No vacuum, no vacuum."

I was so nervous about the outcome of the surgery that I couldn't understand her. I kept hearing her tell me she was going to vacuum out my uterus.

I couldn't figure out why in the world she would take my uterus out, vacuum it, and put it back in! My hands started sweating. I asked Craig to get another nurse to see if she was right.

A new nurse laughed at me and told me it wasn't true, but I didn't believe her. Then my RE came in. I asked *him* if it was true. He just stared at me, and then laughter hit him, too! He bent over, covering his mouth from the sheer thought of my question.

Enough said.

Between my anxiety and the required fasting, I could not comprehend what she meant, which was, "After surgery, you can't vacuum for six weeks."

OHHH!

Laughter was the medicine needed to ease the

tension I felt in my bones.

Author Anne Lamott says in her book, *Bird by Bird*, that she only knows two prayers: "Help me, help me, help me.", and "Thank you, thank you, thank you."

I'm pretty sure the only prayer I said was, "Please, please, please." I'm all for begging in desperate times, and well, this felt pretty desperate.

Dear God, please, please, please let this work, was my plea while being wheeled into the operating room.

I waved goodbye to Craig, wishing he could hold my hand. I would see him in a few hours. This was it. Anxiety about the outcome was in the forefront of my mind, but I believed God was in this.

In the recovery room, I heard a female voice ask me my pain level. I tried to respond, but my throat felt raw. Unable to talk because of having been intubated, I panicked. My eyes wouldn't open. Out of all the warnings they gave me, the doctor failed to mention these.

Adrenaline kicked in. I tried to kick the blankets off to get out of the bed, but shooting pain from my abdomen seared through my body.

A nurse came over and held my hand. My eyes were still refusing to open. I heard her whisper, "Jesus." It was the only word my mind understood. I felt the presence of the Lord so strongly that I relaxed. She told me she was sending someone to get Craig for me. "Just wait a few more minutes, honey," she said. She held my hand while we waited for him.

I opened my eyes to see Craig coming through the curtains. I tried to hold back my tears. I didn't realize I was holding my breath. I wanted to know if it worked. I questioned if it was worth it.

He was grinning from ear to ear. He relayed the news that the surgery was successful. Plus, my eggs and fallopian tubes were in great shape.

The septum was the largest mass of tissue the surgeon had ever seen. The septum took up 90% of my uterus before the surgery, and he was able to remove 95% of it. I wouldn't need two surgeries after all.

Proverbs 12:25 — "Anxiety weighs down the heart, but a kind word cheers it up."

Many emotions overwhelmed my mind—joy, relief, and excitement all rolled into one. Parenthood seemed only a fingertip away!

A little while later, the nurse who held my hand helped me into the car. Outside the hospital doors, she told me she had looked over my chart.

She confided in me, "I prayed for you the whole time you were in recovery, asking the Lord for a baby for you."

She had tried to conceive for sixteen years. After doing IVF, her miracle baby girl was born.

She told us not to give up. Miracles happen, just not in our timeframe.

Her prayers and miracle story infused hope from the depths of my heart to the soles of my feet. She understood my desperation for children. I again had hope that my arms would be full one day. Craig and I drove home glowing.

PERMISSION TO BE BROKEN

Nine days after surgery, I boarded a plane bound for my mama's arms. My RE thought I was crazy for traveling so soon. Once I convinced him I wouldn't bring a carry-on or do any stretching to open the laparoscopic incision in my belly button, he agreed to let me go.

"You are a very strong lady, and you've healed quickly," he said. "You're one of the most positive patients I've ever had. Call me if anything happens."

I took that as a "yes." I made the 2,000-mile flight back home to Ohio. Craig stayed behind for work. It was hard to imagine that two months earlier, we'd had our fourth miscarriage. Here I was with a new lease on life, sort of.

I landed at the airport. My dad picked me up with tears in his eyes. It had been a year since I'd been home, when I'd had my last miscarriage.

When I reached my parents' house, I climbed into my mama's arms. In her bed, I fell apart without warning.

I let myself cry with full abandonment, no withholding of emotions. Being in her arms gave me permission to be broken.

I sobbed from the bottom-of-my-gut. It's a sob that continues to ask all the same frightening questions, knowing there are no answers. It's a sob that says, "No one is judging me right now for not having it together." It's a sob that begs to be understood. It's the sob that wants to be comforted.

These were the tears that only a mama could wipe away. These were the tears I let flow down my face.

Psalm 55:17 — "Evening, morning and noon I cry out in distress, and he hears my voice."

For two weeks I laid in her bed with her. We spent the whole time together watching movies, sharing stories, and making jokes. Nothing had seemed right this past year. The world felt off-kilter. But being home made all the hurt and pain momentarily fade into the background.

In the middle of my trip, much to my chagrin, the incision in my belly button opened. I had zero—I mean ZERO—desire to call my RE to let him know that I ripped open my incision, especially after I had worked so hard to convince him to let me fly home.

So a very spontaneous thought took hold. I grabbed a tiny bottle of superglue and glued my surgical wound shut. But I accidentally glued my entire belly button shut as well!

To my horror, my belly button disappeared! There

was now a straight line where my belly button used to be.

I drove myself to Urgent Care, where a very amused nurse could not contain her laughter.

"Girl, what do you think you are, some kind of superhero? You can't just glue yourself back together and expect a body part to grow back! Next time you gotta call a doctor."

"Yeah, I'm kind of tired of doctors," I laughed with a shrug of my shoulders."

She gave me some antibiotics, and my incision healed by the time the superglue wore out a few weeks later.

After returning from Urgent Care, I sheepishly confessed to my mama what I did. She started laughing uncontrollably. Snorting. Tears streamed down her face; she couldn't catch her breath.

Witnessing her reaction, I couldn't help but burst into laughter myself, almost peeing my pants as I bent over, crossing my legs. My mama shared her own story of a similar incident that happened years earlier. Oh how we made a joyful noise hooting and hollering about our bodies just not doing what we wanted them to do and the medical community scratching their heads at us.

A few nights later, after the superglue debacle, my mom said that we should pray and ask the Lord to show us if my miscarried babies were boys or girls. I honestly thought she was crazy.

I had never heard of people knowing the gender of a miscarried baby. But my mama was a prayer warrior—it was her specialty.

She prayed. I prayed, more out of not wanting to upset her than my being convinced we would find our answers. She believed that if I knew the genders of my babies, then my grieving would lessen.

As she was praying, she told me she saw Jesus rocking my babies, three girls and one boy. I believed the part about Jesus rocking my babies, but I wasn't quite convinced that she was right about the genders. I was skeptical. It seemed a little too weird for me.

She saw my skepticism but wasn't threatened by it.

If I really did have three girls and one boy, not just nameless, genderless babies in Heaven, then why did *Jesus* get to rock them, and *I* didn't?

How unfair!

My momentary jealousy faded. I was comforted just seeing my mama's peace after we prayed. I was a little more at ease too, for some inexplicable reason.

A new conversation opened up for us after my mama saw Jesus holding my babies. She started telling me what it was like to have MS. I never really understood her disease, even though I lived through it for so many years.

I had never seen my mama through the filter of her disease, and neither had she. I knew my mom was an active go-getter before the disease wreaked havoc on her body. She always joked that MS was God's way of telling her to slow down. My parents always put on a happy face about this ugly affliction.

Clearly, it's where I learned to put on my "I'm great!" mask. I never truly saw the toll the disease had taken on my parents until I experienced my own invisible disease of infertility.

That day, I finally caught a glimpse of the internal struggle my mom must have had as she suffered through her own body failing her. Her arms and fingers no longer moved on command. Her legs stopped moving long ago. Her voice was failing, and her lung capacity was shrinking. How frustrating to be a prisoner in your own body! I realized she was holding onto life, trying to keep her brave face in place.

Later that evening, I laid in my childhood bedroom. I had never cleaned out my room when I moved away from my parents' home six years earlier. My room was in a time warp: movie posters still tacked to the ceiling, Teen Bop posters still taped behind my door, knick-knacks from my teenage years still sitting on my bookshelves collecting dust.

Memories flooded my mind.

How many times had I laid on this same bed, staring at this same ceiling, after I'd been grounded for yelling at my mom? How many screaming matches did I get into with her?

Psalm 147:3 — "He heals the brokenhearted and binds up their wounds."

If she had told me what it was like to live in her body, maybe I would have understood and been more patient. Now that the teenage years were over, my mom and I were on the best of terms. My mom and I were finally friends.

Two Pink Lines = Miracle

Six weeks after surgery, we were back at the RE's office. Thankfully my incision wound had healed. I never had to confess my superglue incident to him.

He gave us a calendar, circled the dates, and said, "You've got a green light! Have fun!"

His candor irritated me.

Did he not remember that it took us almost a year to get pregnant with the last baby?

Oozing with skepticism, I told him, "I don't think it's going to be that simple."

"Yeah, but that was before I did my magic. You'll be fine. You'll be pregnant next month," he said offhandedly.

Well, after that statement, I was even more irritated.

What an ego!

Over the course of the next month, I sat in my black rocking chair I had bought fifteen months earlier. A new hope sprung up within me as I poured over Scripture while sitting in my place of remembrance.

I believed our promised baby was coming, but the fear of uncertainty gripped my heart.

Was the surgery really the cure? Did the doctor really do his "magic?"

It had been fifteen months since Rachel called me and told me not to believe what the doctor said and that we were going to have a baby.

As I rocked in my chair, I read biblical accounts of manna falling from the sky, oil and flour not running out, an iron ax head floating, rivers parting, food multiplying, the lame walking, the blind seeing, the deaf hearing, and my personal favorite: women who were once barren birthing children.

It seemed that God liked showing off, defying the odds. Fifteen months earlier, the odds of me having a baby were less than ten percent. Now, according to this doctor, the odds of miscarrying again were slim to none. I liked defying the odds.

It seemed fitting to sit in my rocking chair, recounting God's miracles one by one in Scripture. Once again, I started praising Him for our promised baby as if my arms were already full.

Thank you, Jesus, for answering my prayers. Thank you for giving us a miracle baby.

One night in early fall, just before we left for our church's small group gathering, I felt slightly off. Then it dawned on me,

Could I be pregnant? Do I even dare to hope that I'm pregnant?

I rushed to the bathroom.

Could it be?

Within a few seconds, a double pink line appeared!

We were pregnant with our fifth baby!

"Hey, Babe!" I shouted. "Oh my god, look!" I held up the pregnancy test.

Craig's eyes bulged from his sockets. He knew well what a double line meant. We both started jumping up and down, hugging each other. We were overjoyed and couldn't contain our excitement! We thought it would take months to get pregnant, like it had before.

> *Ecclesiastes 3:1,4 — "There is a time for everything, and a season for every activity under the heavens: ...a time to weep and a time to laugh, a time to mourn and a time to dance."*

I was instantly in planning mode. Where would we put the crib? What would our baby look like? Where would this baby go to school? What kind of career would they have?

I dove headfirst into dreaming!

At our small group gathering, we waited until the end of the night when Foster asked if there were any prayer requests.

"We're pregnant!" we announced. Our whole group overflowed with joy! Everyone there was happy for us. They knew how much we had been through.

That night, we prayed for this baby to make it into our arms. Both fear and excitement ran through my blood. The next month would be our most dangerous month, if the past were to repeat itself. We wanted all the prayers we could get.

A few years earlier, when we found out we were pregnant the first time, we chose to follow the traditional timeframe and keep our pregnancy a secret.

However, that backfired when I miscarried. I needed to talk about my miscarriage, but I felt strange talking about it when my close friends didn't know I was pregnant in the first place. It was hard for others to "mourn with those who mourn" when they weren't offered the privilege to "rejoice with those who rejoice."

Not being able to process my emotions out loud with women after my other miscarriages made me decide that I'd rather people know we were pregnant, even if we miscarried again. I personally needed their prayers more than I needed secrets and traditions.

I cherished people's prayers. I coveted their prayers. I believed that the more people we had petitioning God, the more our prayers would be answered. The Bible says that God hears our individual prayers. I wanted everyone I knew to pray for us.

Psalm 139:14 — "I praise you because I am fearfully and wonderfully made; your works are wonderful, I know that full well."

I did not want to lose this baby.

Is this our baby we named "Praise" so long ago? Is this baby our Mikayla Hope?

I was both full of joy and apprehension. My heart

was full, yet guarded. I didn't want it to break again.

I can't handle another miscarriage, Jesus. Please let this baby live, I begged.

Craig and I praised the Lord in our uncertainty. Our promised baby was growing within me.

Thank you, Jesus, for answering our prayers!

A WALKING
CONUNDRUM

I called the RE's office to tell them I was pregnant. They didn't seem concerned. "Let's schedule an appointment for next week," the receptionist said nonchalantly.

I couldn't believe she wasn't trying to get me in sooner. Panic gripped me.

What if I miscarry before then?

I was on a first-name basis with her. She knew my history. I reminded her of my previous track record of two miscarriages early in the first trimester. The receptionist transferred me to the nurse, who gave me a prescription for progesterone. Calmness ensued.

Okay, at least there's a plan.

My first indication of a miracle came a week later. I was still pregnant; no complications had occurred. A sigh of relief flowed through my body.

The day of our appointment arrived. The doctor greeted us both with hugs in the hallway. "Congratulations, you two! See, I told you you'd be pregnant next month," he said with a twinkle in his eye.

"Yeah, you did, and I didn't believe you!" I chuckled as I hugged him back.

In the exam room, the ultrasound machine was on. The doctor looked throughout my uterus via the screen but couldn't find the pregnancy sac. "Hmm..." he murmured.

Oh, this isn't good.

Fear encompassed my heart. Memories of this exact scenario fifteen months earlier replayed in my mind.

A few moments later, he found it. "Oh, *there* you are," he said to the screen.

Goodness gracious, that scared me!

I didn't realize I was holding my breath.

That took a little too long for my comfort.

"The pregnancy sac has implanted in the best possible location in your uterus," he said.

The sac had implanted far from the scar tissue from the surgery, as well as far from other tissue that was there.

"By the end of next week, we will hear a heart-beat!" he said.

Thank you, Jesus!

We had never heard any of our babies' heartbeats before.

Could I hold my breath and be full of hope at the same time?

I was a walking conundrum. I prayed and begged and praised and prayed and begged all week.

Thank you, Jesus, for this baby! You are awesome! Please let us hear a heartbeat!

Morning sickness was in full swing, but even with

past pregnancies, I was still vomiting while I was miscarrying, so I wasn't comforted by that. I just had to sit and wait for the minutes to turn into hours and the hours to turn into days. The wait was agonizing.

Psalm 27:14 — "Wait for the LORD; be strong and take heart and wait for the LORD."

In the book, *The Gifts of Imperfection,* Dr. Brené Brown says, "Joy is the most vulnerable emotion we experience, and if you cannot tolerate joy, what you do is you start dress rehearsing tragedy."

I was so scared that I would miscarry in the week waiting for a heartbeat that my joy was kidnapped, waiting for tragedy.

At the same time, I was learning to look to Jesus in a way I had never known before. I was waiting with bated breath. Waiting while pregnant was new territory for me. I only knew how to wait for a miscarriage, never for a healthy pregnancy.

God was patiently developing in me a deep trust that could only be built while I couldn't see what was happening within me.

THE STRAIN OF FAITH

The countdown of days until we would be able to hear a heartbeat dragged on. Each hour of expecting to see signs of a miscarriage and yet believing everything would be fine created tension between my mind and spirit.

The strain of faith and trust and doubt and disbelief played a tug-of-war on my heart as if Heaven held onto one side and Hell gripped the other.

Seven days passed. Each day ended with a sigh of relief as my head hit the pillow.

I'm still pregnant.

The morning arrived for the next ultrasound. Craig and I both held our breath as I lay on the exam table waiting for the doctor to say something.

Would we see a heartbeat?

Without warning or fanfare, the most wonderful sound our ears had ever heard flooded the room. We knew what it meant.

The rhythmic swooshing sound of life in me! There was our peanut on the black and white and gray screen.

I choked back tears. It was the first heartbeat we had ever heard. Craig held my hand and gave it a squeeze. Our promised baby was here. In seven and a half months, our arms would be full!

Job 37:5 — "God's voice thunders in marvelous ways; he does great things beyond our understanding."

The nurse standing by the door whispered something to our doctor, but I didn't quite hear what she said.

"Yes," he answered her with excitement in his voice, "This is the patient who had the largest septum I have ever seen and who had four miscarriages!"

Although I didn't recognize her, she knew me. Apparently, she was the same nurse who assisted during the failed HSG procedure four months earlier.

Now our baby was serenading us with a precious heartbeat.

I looked at the nurse. Our eyes met. A connection took place between us, woman to woman. My voice couldn't find the right words to say, but she understood what my eyes whispered.

All of the pain was worth it; Miracles do happen.

She nodded her head with a knowing smile. A smile spread across my face, too, as I looked back toward the screen. Yes, my promised baby was coming!

After seeing and hearing our little one's heartbeat, I felt so much peace. I could breathe again. No cramping or bleeding had occurred—a huge milestone for us!

> *Psalm 71:23 — "My lips will shout*
> *for joy when I sing praise to you—I*
> *whom you have delivered."*

Our house was filled with joy!

Thank you, Jesus!

The days no longer felt like years, but minutes. I no longer expected to see death in my womb. My world was a little brighter. This was what the other side of pain felt like. The wet blanket of sorrow lifted from my shoulders.

My tightened chest was now released, allowing me to inhale the deep joy of hearing and believing good news. True, faith-filled joy entered my heart. This baby was coming! Hope was alive! We would meet our little one soon!

No Words to Pray

I woke up in the early hours of the morning—bleeding.

Not again, God! Not again! How could this be happening?

I laid in bed, not wanting to move. I couldn't believe it.

Why in the world was this happening again?

I called into work and took the day off. I had no words to pray. I stuffed my tears into the deep recesses of my heart. I didn't want to cry. It just didn't seem worth it.

I called my doctor's office as soon as it opened. "I'm miscarrying," I said.

The receptionist asked, "How soon can you get here?"

Craig and I drove in silence. Sorrow hung over our heads for the entire 60-minute drive. We sat in the car as if we were in a funeral procession on the freeway. The world seemed to be moving in slow motion as we inched our way through LA traffic.

Once we arrived at the doctor's office, they rushed us into a room. We didn't even wait in the lobby. After four hours, the bleeding had not stopped, but had slowed down.

The doctor started the ultrasound. Immediately, we saw the heartbeat of our nugget. Our baby was still there. Shock stung my eyes and spread to the tips of my toes.

"What? I'm still pregnant!?" I wailed.

Relief filled every fiber of my being.

How in the world am I still pregnant?

It was the best news I'd ever heard. "Oh thank God!" I sighed.

The doctor wasn't quite sure why I was bleeding. He said I needed to take it easy for the rest of the day. If I saw tissue or started cramping, I was to call him right away. I realized that those were two signs I didn't see or feel. I started laughing.

I knew what a miscarriage was, and this was not it! Bleeding without the signs of tissue or cramping most likely meant everything was fine, but I had never only bled before. I was not told that bleeding was normal. I only knew death, not life. It was new territory to think that a child was growing within me, that a baby was being fed by my womb. I was learning to walk by faith and not by sight.

They did more HCG bloodwork to compare levels and sent me home to prop up my feet. A technician called me later that afternoon with the results of my bloodwork. Everything looked great. "Your levels keep rising like they should," she said. "There is nothing to worry about."

WHERE IS COMPASSION?

A week later, I was still spotting morning, noon, and night. Every time I saw blood, I panicked, *"I'm miscarrying."*

I prayed under my breath every second of every day. The Apostle Paul said to pray without ceasing, and I was doing just that.

"God, I'm clinging to hope even when my eyes cannot see," I proclaimed in those moments.

Instead of seeing the RE once a week, we started seeing him twice a week. He did an ultrasound at each appointment. At our nine-week appointment, blood was found inside the pregnancy sac.

The prognosis was devastating. "If blood continues to fill the pregnancy sac, you will miscarry," he said softly.

It was the first time I saw concern on his face. He suggested we do another ultrasound in two days.

I didn't believe him. *Denial.*

There is no way we are going to miscarry; we've come so far!

If hope was a balloon that I was learning to release

into the sky, it popped right in front of me. Our baby was drowning in blood, and there was nothing we could do about it...but pray.

I sent out an email to our friends in our little church, asking for prayer. I felt so helpless.

God gave us a promise, and yet this baby might not be that promise. I tried to put on a brave face, but inside, I was a wreck. All I wanted to do was hide my head under the bed covers.

Could we just have one good day, God? Can I ever be pregnant without complications? Without any worry, God? You. Gave. Us. This. Baby.

I kept reciting from Isaiah 55: "So is my word that goes out from my mouth: It will not return to me empty, but will accomplish what I desire and achieve the purpose for which I sent it."

It seemed cruel to give us hope and then take it away...again. It seemed cruel to let us be pregnant for nine weeks just to lose this baby, too. Depression took hold. I called my mama. She prayed that this baby would pull through. She prayed that the blood would disappear.

Craig didn't know how to handle me. I was inconsolable. I wanted to die. Heaven seemed to be a better place than this earth. I had clung to hope so tightly, but it was dashed again.

My baby. Drowning. In blood. I chose to be open with a church lady about what was going on. I wanted all the prayers I could get. She kindly asked, "Well, are you praying or reading your Bible?"

I reeled from the verbal blow. I stepped away from her.

Are you kidding me? All I need to do is pray and read my Bible!?

No words came out of my mouth. I couldn't believe the admonishment thrown my way, even if it was said in a kind tone. If I read my Bible and prayed, would that mean that my heart wouldn't experience sorrow every time the toilet paper had blood on it?

Clearly, she had not read the book of Psalms, ever. King David would praise God, then ask if God had forgotten him, then offer praise again. My life was one long Psalm-cycle—not just with this pregnancy, but throughout my entire journey with infertility and miscarriages.

*Psalm 77:3 — "I remembered you,
God, and I groaned; I meditated, and
my spirit grew faint."*

I didn't know how to respond. She was not the first person to say something like that to me in our little church. I felt slapped in the face. If she only knew how much I had begged God to keep this baby. If she only knew my heart.

If I only knew how to articulate my emotions better, maybe she wouldn't have said that.

I was learning who I could share my struggles with. Unfortunately, the list was getting smaller. My walls were getting thicker. I didn't know who to trust until the trust was broken.

This would be the last time I shared openly about my heart breaking every time I saw a sign of a miscarriage looming. It was a lot easier to believe in a miracle when others were believing for it right along with me, but it was devastating when my *supposed* support system did not believe.

---

2 Corinthians 1:4 — "[God] comforts us in all our troubles, so that we can comfort those in any trouble with the comfort we ourselves receive from God."

My heart needed compassion. My anxiety needed a Savior. My mind needed to know God was in control. Compassion and a simple prayer were needed in my time of mourning over our devastating news. I wished for a hug. I wished for a prayer for a miracle. I wished a compassionate response of, "I'm so sorry," would have been given, or "Let's pray this baby in to your arms."

Oh, how I wished for a moment of solidarity instead of the offer of a religious to-do list to mend my broken heart.

HOPE
CHALLENGED

Two days later, we drove back to the RE's office, not knowing the fate of our baby. I laid on the table, holding my breath. Craig held my hand. Squinting my eyes at the screen as the doctor moved around the ultrasound wand, I couldn't see the pregnancy sac at all.

"There it is!" he exclaimed, discovering the sac just as I began to panic. "The blood is gone!"

Craig and I squeezed our hands together. We looked at the screen and then back at each other. I exhaled a loud sigh of relief.

It's a miracle! Our baby is still here.

By 12 weeks, I'd been to 18 doctor's appointments. I'd had 13 ultrasounds and countless vials of blood drawn. By all standards, my pregnancy was high-risk.

Every day, hope was hidden in a different way. The days I spotted became fewer and fewer. I prayed under my breath and clasped my hands together, trying to combat my fear.

When there were no complications, I would breathe a sigh of relief and lift my hands in praise.

Clinging to a hidden hope was more of a challenge than I had ever realized. I knew God was in the miracle business, but I didn't know this was a battle for my mind as well as my hope.

I didn't know that clinging to hope would defy the odds just as much as having a miracle baby would.

A new vigor of hope and faith strengthened my resolve. I wondered if I was in denial or just full of trust.

Either way, I was learning that hope was a choice. I'd rather hope than succumb to depression. "This baby is coming. This is our promised child," I frequently said.

Holding on to hope was more life-giving than holding on to fear. I was sick of living in fear. I knew this baby within me was a miracle. A little baby bump was starting to show the world that God loved defying the odds, too. Hope was on the rise.

Then, without any warning, history repeated itself yet again. As I was getting ready for bed one Sunday evening, I went to the bathroom. Blood gushed into the toilet. The water in the toilet bowl turned bright red. I gasped. My heart stopped. Paralyzing fear spread over me.

Without a conscious decision, I started counting the seconds aloud with my hand over my mouth, "1, 2, 3, 4..."

As if someone turned on a water faucet, blood gushed for ten full seconds. Then, as fast as it started, it stopped. It was more blood than I had ever seen before with any miscarriage.

I immediately walked into our bedroom and laid

on our bed. With shaky hands, I called into work to let them know I wasn't coming in the next day.

I didn't see any tissue. I haven't lost my baby yet, but what if there isn't a heartbeat?

In the midst of my panic, peace filled our bedroom. The shaking in my body stopped. I had learned from past pregnancies that peace only meant God was with me; it didn't mean that everything would turn out the way I wanted it to. An inexplicable peace filled me. God was with me, no matter the outcome.

My eyes saw what my mind could not deny. This was not normal. Something was deadly wrong.

This can't be the end. This can't be what God has for me! I was made to be a mama. This baby is not going anywhere.

There was a holy stubbornness. A holy resolve to push through and believe for a miracle.

Romans 4:17b — "...God...gives life to the dead and calls into being things that were not."

Yet, I kept imagining a lifeless baby on the ultrasound screen.

This is not the end of my story. It can't be. God, you have spoken. You don't give up. Jesus isn't through with me, yet.

God had more plans for me. I just knew it. I wasn't ready to give up. However, that same image of a lifeless baby floating in my womb kept replaying in my mind.

"Jesus! Help me!" I cried.

The mental battle for hope and faith continued well into the night.

A NEW DEFINITION
OF STRENGTH

I prepared for the news that we had miscarried. My bleeding had turned to spotting, but it had not stopped completely. I had no emotion.

At the RE's office, I lay on the exam table waiting for the news. I couldn't bring myself to look at the ultrasound screen. It was too painful to hope.

The doctor said, "Linni, look."

I dared to turn my head towards the screen. As I did, he turned on the sound. There was our little baby's heartbeat.

Lub-dub, lub-dub, lub-dub

Our baby was healthy and whole. I exhaled a sigh of relief.

Thank you, Jesus!

The doctor didn't hold back his relief, either. He had no idea why I kept bleeding so much. It was wonderful seeing him root for us.

Craig and I shared a silent, teary-eyed moment as he squeezed my hand. This baby was coming. Our faith grew in strength that day.

However, after this scare, my emotions were still

on a roller coaster. I felt like I was going crazy. One minute I could praise God with full confidence that this baby was coming, and the next, I would steel myself for the devastating news that this baby, just like the others, would not make it either.

Psalm 116:1 — "I love the LORD, for he heard my voice; he heard my cry for mercy."

With my emotions all over the place, it was becoming difficult to trust the church ladies I'd thought I could trust. I had gotten a slap in the face when I was honest and shared my anxious heart in the past.

If I can't be honest in church, then I don't want any part of it.

I told Craig I was done with church. I felt like I had to be perfect. Say the right things. Do the right things. It was just too exhausting.

Nonetheless, my perfect exterior attitude was in place. Anyone who asked how I was doing was told that I found life to be wonderful. My resolute demeanor came more from *deciding* to believe my own words than from *actually* believing them.

I wasn't going to be fooled again. I would not share what was really going on in my heart. The walls around my heart grew thicker and taller. I was the city of Jericho, tall and proud. No one could get in, and no one would be allowed to stay.

My saving grace was that we were already committed to working in the church's Sunday school class. I loved seeing the kids each week. It became my escape, my safe haven from the older women's prying eyes and their never-ending admonishments.

One Sunday, a little girl came skipping up to me and handed me a note. She hugged my neck and ran back to play with the other little girls. I unfolded the note, written on a torn-off corner of a notebook paper. As soon as I read the words, I stuffed the note in my back pocket before anyone could catch a glimpse of the tears that dared to fall.

Driving home a few hours later, I pulled the note out of my back pocket. I read the girl's words again in her little eight-year-old handwriting, misspellings and all:

dear Miss. Craig and Mr. Linie.
I am parrying for ur baby.

I clutched the note to my chest and breathed out a little prayer. Faith like a child. If she could believe this baby was going to make it, so could I.

> *Matthew 19:14 — "Jesus said, 'Let the little children come to me, and do not hinder them, for the kingdom of heaven belongs to such as these.'"*

Help me stay strong, Lord, I prayed.

Strong. My terrible definition: No tears. No emotion. A pillar of strength. Head held high. Having a scripture at the ready to parrot back to someone when they asked how I was doing. I heard God say to my heart,

"I don't want you to be strong your way. I want people to see your heart. Keep it open.
Keep telling people that you believe Me for this baby. That's real strength."

There was something about knowing a child was praying for my miracle baby that caused a confidence, an expectation, and a faith to grow in my heart during the beginning of my second trimester.

That little girl's note did more than I could have ever imagined. It took what little hope I had left and made it grow exponentially.

It would be six weeks of waiting until the next scheduled ultrasound.

I was given the privilege of seeing this baby grow from a bean to a nugget to a little one with moving arms and legs throughout the first trimester. God met me in my uncertainty by letting me have so many ultrasounds. In my fear and in my anxiety, He showed Himself faithful and kind. I started seeing gifts all around me.

Psalm 145:17 — "The LORD is
righteous in all his ways and faithful
in all he does."

Could it be that all of the bleeding and heartache

throughout the first trimester were a gift in disguise?

All of the ultrasounds were a way to see inside my womb. I had wished for Superman's x-ray vision, and two times a week my wish was granted, albeit at the cost of heart palpitations and sweaty hands. Regardless, the gift was being unwrapped.

Each time I panicked, I saw God hold me—a gift I would not have experienced if there had never been heartache. The gift of comfort. The gift of faith being formed. The gift of grace found in weakness. These gifts were priceless commodities, ones that could easily be stolen away by fear if not protected by the choice of holding onto hope.

> *2 Corinthians 12:9a — ... "My grace is sufficient for you, for my power is made perfect in weakness."*

My imperfect emotions were making space for God's grace to flow into my uncertainty.

ONE LITTLE GIRL

I sat in my interpreting chair at work, facing my high school students. In just a few hours, Craig and I would find out the gender of our little baby. The clock couldn't move fast enough. My brain was split into way too many directions, causing sloppy multitasking to take place.

One of my students caught me in mid-daydream, wondering if the ultrasound would detect any physical deformities or heart problems in my little one.

"Are you thinking about your baby?" he asked.

"Yes, yes, I am," I replied, bringing myself back to the classroom.

"I bet it's going to be a boy. You're really good at dealing with us guys, but you're terrible with the girls."

A more direct truth had never been spoken. I *was* better at managing teenage-boy antics than the catty drama of teenage girls.

Oh Lord, this baby better be a boy. He's right. I'm gonna mess up a little girl!

The bell rang. Class was dismissed. I grabbed my

purse and headed to the parking lot.

Our perinatologist, a high-risk pregnancy special-ist, would be doing the 18-week ultrasound. I was meeting Craig at the doctor's office, but first I needed to navigate through LA traffic. I sat in my car on the stop-and-go 101 freeway, one of the most congested freeways in all of Los Angeles.

The drive without traffic would have taken 40 minutes; with traffic, it would take at least 60-90 minutes. Such a long way to see a specialist in a sea of red tail lights. It was such a long journey forward, counting the exits until I found the one I needed. A long way for anxiety to rise in my heart as the minutes ticked closer and closer to the appointment time.

Jesus, I can't miss this appointment. The traffic has got to move!

It was as if God parted the traffic just as He did the Red Sea. The cars started picking up their pace. I finally had my foot on the accelerator. My heartbeat slowed down, and a little prayer of "Thank you" parted my lips.

I'm going to make it!

I arrived at the doctor's office with two minutes to spare. I spotted Craig reading a magazine while he waited for me. Feeling flustered from traffic, I sat down and took a deep breath while I pulled a piece of hair back into my ponytail that had escaped in my mad dash to the office.

The nurse called my name. Craig and I were led back to a darkened room down the hallway. We knew the routine. This would be our 15th ultrasound in 18 weeks.

A woman started the ultrasound. She asked if we wanted to know the gender.

"Yes! We do!" We both exclaimed.

Without any fanfare or personality, she said, "It's a girl."

What?

I was shocked. My eyes were huge!

The name we picked out so long ago would actually be for this baby?

The ultrasound tech asked if the baby had a name. Before she even finished her question, Craig interrupted her and said, "Her name will be Mikayla Hope. We've been praying for this baby for years. After four miscarriages, she's here!"

Curiosity piqued, she turned from the screen and asked, "Does the name have a meaning?"

Without hesitation, Craig told her our story of Mikayla meaning praise. He told how when we picked the name years earlier, we were going to praise God for a baby that wasn't in our arms yet, but that we believed would be.

All of a sudden, I felt inadequate to carry this little girl.

My own mom and I didn't have the best of relationships when I was a teenager; how in the world am I going to be a good mama to a girl?

As quickly as those thoughts entered my brain, praise pushed them out.

God gave me this baby. Thank you, God, for this baby! At least they start out as little infants and not teenagers! We'll learn together, I'm sure. Thank you, Jesus, for Mikayla Hope. She'll be here soon! I can do this.

A little pep talk to myself and praise to my God spilled from my heart.

Psalm 34:1 — "I will extol the LORD
at all times; his praise will always be
on my lips."

Still lying on the exam table with warm gooey gel on my belly, I saw our little girl on the ultrasound screen. *Mikayla Hope.* I was pregnant with a little girl named Mikayla Hope!

I could say her name a thousand times and never get tired of it. Mikayla Hope means, "Who is like our God?" The answer? No one. No one else could give us this baby but our God! No one. We were having a girl!

HOPE'S
GRAVEYARD

When my morning sickness, or all-day sickness, didn't end in the first trimester, I was diagnosed with Hyperemesis Gravidarum—a fancy medical term for puking around the clock.

Every time I ran to the toilet, even if it was in the middle of the night, I would hug the toilet bowl saying, "Thank you, Jesus!"

After all we had been through, there was no way I was going to complain about throwing up. I even learned how to keep my eyes open while vomiting and driving on the freeway!

However, at 22 weeks pregnant, it was taking its toll on my body. I woke up Friday morning with extreme lethargy and a fever. I decided to stay home from work.

While sitting on my couch in a pink turtleneck maternity sweater, my phone rang. It was the doctor's office. My bloodwork was in from a routine draw. The screening showed some concerns.

The physician's assistant asked, "Can you come in right away for us to draw more blood?"

My heartbeat quickened. My hand holding the phone tightened to the point where my knuckles turned white. "You mean, like, right now?" I asked in a panic.

"Yes, as soon as you can. Since it's Friday, we close early."

"I can be there in twenty minutes."

"Okay, we'll let the receptionist know to bring you immediately back to my office."

What in the world is going on?

My heart was strangled in anxiety, threatening to bulge from my chest.

I grabbed my coat and keys and ran as fast as I could to my car.

I'm not going to call Craig. It will just worry him more. I don't even know what's going on yet. Please, God, let everything be okay.

Psalm 28:2a — "Hear my cry for mercy as I call to you for help."

I sped through traffic, thankful that I had taken the day off work. If I had been at work, I would have missed this important call. Grateful for God's timing, I walked through the double doors of the hospital and made my way to the doctor's office down the hall. When I said my name to the receptionist, she motioned to the door and said to follow the winding hallway around to the back office.

What? They're not going to wait for a nurse to guide me there? Oh no, this must be really bad.

I walked into the PA's office. She had a form already filled out for me.

"Hi there," she greeted me, "I'm so sorry to worry you on the phone. Thank you for coming in on such short notice."

She continued gravely, "Your bloodwork shows signs of RH antibodies. We need to double-check to see if these antibodies have increased."

I burst into a full-body cold sweat, remembering that the midwife told me about this possibility last summer. My heart jumped into my throat. Tears threatened to fall. I swallowed hard before I spoke.

"Can my baby die if they have an increase?" I asked, trying to hold it together.

Not directly answering my question, she replied, "It would hinder future pregnancies from progressing. We won't know until we do more bloodwork."

"But, can my baby die?" I asked again, trying to keep my calm exterior from betraying my decaying composure.

"Like I said, we won't know that until we see your results. Your RH antibodies are very high. This could cause *complications* for your baby, but we can discuss more options on Monday when we get your results, okay?" She said this without a hint of optimism in her voice.

The only word my mind registered was "complications." I took the form and walked across the hall to get my blood drawn with tears streaming down my face.

This is it. My baby is going to die from these stupid RH antibodies. How in the world could you let this happen, God? How could you do this to me? You let me get this far, and then this baby dies, too?

I watched as the nurse put the needle in my arm. The blood dripping into the four large vials held my fate.

The day before my 25th birthday, I find out that my baby could die. What a way to celebrate turning a quarter of a century old.

Please God, please change this! Please do something! Anything!

Psalm 119:156 — "Your compassion, LORD, is great; preserve my life according to your laws."

I, of course, did what all people do after they hear a vague diagnosis. I went home and googled what high levels of RH antibodies in the second trimester meant.

What I found made my body lose feeling in all of my extremities. My skin turned pale. My mind spun out of focus. "...[E]xisting antibodies could destroy red blood cells, causing Hemolytic disease and in rare cases, death."

According to my instant medical degree from my Google search, RH antibodies meant that my baby would need a blood transfusion. But, 22 weeks was too early in the gestation period for a transfusion. We would have to sit around and wait for Mikayla Hope to grow and possibly do a blood transfusion around 28 weeks, if she survived the wait.

All I had to see was the word "death." I sent an

email to our church friends asking for prayer. I called my friend, Michelle, who was planning on taking me out to breakfast in the morning for my birthday. I updated her on the events of the afternoon. "I can't make it. I need to cancel tomorrow," I said.

"Okay, but don't you want us to be with you through this?" she half-asked, half-begged.

"No, I just want to be alone," I whispered, trying to hold back tears.

After a few more questions and comments, she convinced me to have breakfast in the morning. The idea of celebrating while so many unknowns hung over my head was enough to shut down all hope that gave peace to my soul.

My baby could die. For real. A true life-threatening condition could be developing, all because of medical negligence in past pregnancies that went unchecked for RH antibodies.

I felt nothing but darkness. If there was a graveyard somewhere that kept my hope buried, it was in my heart. Waiting until Monday would be the longest weekend of my life. But, God had a miracle up His sleeve.

A FRIEND LOVES AT ALL TIMES

I woke up the next morning—Saturday morning—to the sun's rays shining into my bedroom window.

It's my 25th birthday. I should be excited, but instead, I just want to stay in bed forever.

I laid on my back with the blankets up under my chin, staring at the ceiling, feeling my baby kick.

Without warning, a hurricane of anger hit me from all sides. My insides were drowning in the most torrential downpour of anger and turmoil.

Jeremiah 20:18 — "Why did I ever come out of the womb to see trouble and sorrow and to end my days in shame?"

Each tiny kick that morning was a painful reminder that what should be the most joyous feeling in the world—to feel little feet against my insides—had become an assault on my raw emotions.

How many more kicks will I feel until she's gone?

Instead of each kick being met with thanksgiving, it was met with cursing.

How could a good God let this *&$# happen? Do you really want me to praise you for this? Because that ain't gonna happen.

I reluctantly met my friends for my birthday breakfast at a little café in Old Town. Anger burned in my belly.

I had grown up hearing that a Christian wasn't supposed to be angry, let alone cuss. But then what? Was I supposed to be happy instead? I didn't know that anger was a stage of grief or that this had anything to do with grief at all. I just knew that my trusty 'ol companion, the "I'm great!" mask, was back on.

I ordered an omelet. I told my three friends sitting around the table about the diagnosis from the day before, trying to process what was going on. Each word spoken left me feeling more raw, more exposed, and more aware of how little control I had.

I played with my food, desperately trying to paint a smile on my face. I didn't have an appetite. The only place I wanted to be was in the safety of my own bed with the covers over my head.

We asked for the check and made our way down the street to the car. Michelle drove us all back to her place. I sat in the car quietly.

It's so nice of them to take time out of their day to have breakfast with me, but I can't stop making this so awkward. No one knows what to say, and I don't even know what I want them to say. Can this day just be over?

We walked to Michelle's front door. It swung open wide.

"SURPRISE!"

There was our entire small group in Michelle's living room, jumping out from all corners to celebrate this *horrible* birthday. Streamers and balloons were everywhere. Craig, along with Michelle and her husband, Foster, had been planning this surprise party for weeks, and here I was trying to cancel it.

Go figure. No wonder why she was trying everything in her power to keep me from canceling.

I had no clue. I was shocked. My good 'ol companion, the mask, fell off. Tears streamed down my face.

Proverbs 17:17a — "A friend loves at all times..."

People are rooting for us. They're believing for this baby right along with us. We're going to make it, we have to! With a room full of people praying for this baby to make it to our arms, how could we not? It's just gotta turn out okay.

LIGHTNING
STRIKES

The following morning, I walked into the back of the church's auditorium. I found a seat close to the exit in case I needed to run if tears threatened to fall. Since Craig was at work, I was alone.

I hated sitting by myself in church. I felt so alone in all of my anguish.

Why can't Craig just be here with me?

Even with a surprise birthday party the day before, I was still consumed with fear. The kindness of friends only staves off anxiety for so long. Fear that my baby wouldn't make it paralyzed my hope.

Fear took over my thoughts like a dark fog on a treacherous road. Fear that Craig wouldn't know how to handle me if things got worse caused me to keep to myself. Fear that this diagnosis was just the beginning of more heartache to come ate away at my resolve to praise.

A few songs into the worship time, one of the pastors jumped up on stage and said, "I believe God wants to heal some colds today. Raise your hand if you have a cold."

This is out of the ordinary.

I couldn't remember the last time something like that had been said or if it had ever been said in this little church.

What the heck, if God can heal a cold, He can heal my baby and me, too.

I raised my hand for prayer.

Psalm 143:1 — "LORD, hear my prayer, listen to my cry for mercy; in your faithfulness and righteousness come to my relief."

I didn't know what to expect, but I did know that if the Bible is true and people were healed in the Bible, and if God is the same yesterday, today, and forever, then that meant that the same God from the Bible is the same God today. He can heal people today just as he did thousands of years ago.

As the pastor prayed for people to be healed of their colds, I felt the strangest sensation. A powerful electric current ran instantaneously from the top of my head to the tips of my toes.

In less than a millisecond, the sensation of being touched by lightning zapped me and then vanished before I even realized what had happened.

In my spirit, I knew Jesus had put His powerful hand on me right in the middle of all of my questioning, my doubting, and my wondering if He was even good. I had never had an experience with Him in that way before.

Jesus interrupted my thoughts. My worries. My anxiety. My fear. He touched me. Not because I was a good, perfect Christian, but because He moves in our pain. He proves Himself alive, real, and full of love.

Psalm 118:1 — "Give thanks to the LORD, for he is good; his love endures forever."

I knew right then and there that I was healed. My baby was healed. I didn't know whether to scream, cry, or shout for joy. I just sat there in stunned silence. For the first time in two days, a real smile spread across my face.

After the church service, the same pastor came over to me. "I'm so sorry to hear the news about your baby," he said.

I wanted to tell him I believed Jesus healed me, even though I didn't have a cold. I wanted to say, *"I still raised my hand for prayer anyway!"*

But nothing came from my lips. Would he laugh at me if I told him I believed God had healed me? Would he tell me God just heals minor things and the big stuff is left up to surgeons, doctors, and specialists?

I didn't know how he would react if I told him I was healed, especially since I didn't have any proof. All I had was a feeling that my body was different.

After church, I walked to my car. For the first time in the 48 hours since the devastating phone call from my doctor's office, I was confident and full of peace.

WAITING FOR THE CALL

Monday came and went. I called the doctor's office twice to see if my test results were in from my bloodwork. Each time the answer was, "No, call back in a few hours."

I expected such waiting to take its toll on me or for panic to arise—my normal roller coaster—but there was an indescribable peace in me. A peace that only comes from above. A peace that can't be created. A peace that can't be destroyed. A peace that truly surrounded me. I knew a miracle had occurred the day before, and I was just waiting for confirmation.

I fell asleep Monday night without hearing from the doctor.

Philippians 4:7 — "And the peace of God, which transcends all understanding, will guard your hearts and your minds in Christ Jesus."

It was as if all the cycles of bad news, good news,

and bad news had actually had a purpose. I had gone through training. My hope was no longer in my circumstances, but in my God.

Charles Spurgeon, a preacher and theologian, said, "My faith rests not in what I am, or shall be, or feel, or know, but in what Christ is, in what He has done, and in what He is doing for me."

The bad news of antibodies being built up in my body, causing possible issues for my baby, just couldn't be the end of my story. We had come too far.

The encounter I'd had with Jesus the day before—the moment of feeling touched by God, the power of a split-second transformation from worry and panic into complete peace—stoked up faith in my inner being. God is a good God who desires good for us. In the midst of so many unknowns, this truth started to permeate my mind.

Psalm 23:4 — "Even though I walk through the darkest valley, I will fear no evil, for you are with me; your rod and your staff, they comfort me."

Tuesday morning, I received my long-awaited phone call while at work. I picked up my phone and excused myself from the classroom.

Once in the hall, I asked the nurse to repeat herself. "Your bloodwork came back. We didn't find antibodies in your blood," she said.

"What?!" I shouted, and then quickly covered my mouth, shocked by the news. "What do you mean there weren't any antibodies found? How could that be?" I asked in astonishment.

"Ma'am, I don't know what to say, it's a miracle. I don't know what else to tell you. We've never seen this before."

I hung up the phone with her words, "It's a miracle," ringing in my ears.

"It's a miracle!" I whispered to myself, wanting to shout for joy, but refraining because classes were in session. *God healed every part of me—my blood and all!*

The nurse said it was a miracle.

How many medical professionals say that?

DENIAL OR
FAITH?

Heading into the third trimester with our miracle baby growing within me was a physical reminder of a spiritual principle. One doesn't see one's faith growing in them until it's needed the most. My baby was growing. I was growing. My hope and faith in a loving God, who loves at all times, was growing, too.

On a routine visit to our perinatologist, the doctor discovered that Mikayla Hope had a hole in her heart. He said she would need surgery as soon as she was born. There were also signs of preterm labor.

For the first time in years of struggling to conceive, miscarrying four babies, and now being pregnant with our fifth baby, I did not panic when I heard the report. In fact, I surprised myself with my own reaction. I believed the doctor was overreacting.

He seems to have forgotten how many miracles it took just for us to get this far in our pregnancy. My baby is fine.

Faith grew where I least expected it to, right in the middle of heartache, chaos, and stormy weather. My faith was firmly planted in Jesus, not my circumstances.

Could the emotional roller coaster have finally paid off? Could it be that all the heartache has prepared me to stay calm in the storm now?

The doctor's words didn't even phase me. God spoke years ago that we were going to have a baby, and this baby was coming with a whole heart. I was sure of it.

The perinatologist put me on a special diet to see if we could regulate some of the preterm labor. I begrudgingly agreed. The diet allowed for no—I mean absolutely no—carbs at all. Not one iota.

On one hand, I was willing to do anything to have this baby. On the other hand, I thought the doctor was being absolutely ridiculous. I mean, why can't a girl eat some bread and crackers, for heaven's sake?

I walked out of the office without batting an eye at the news. I was unaware of my silent victory until days later, when the doctor's words hit me, *"Your baby could be in the hospital for a few weeks if you don't follow this plan."*

I realized I had not panicked yet. Uncharacteristically, I continued about my days as if there was nothing wrong. Not an ounce of panic invaded my heart. Some would call this denial. I knew it was faith.

A PROMISE
BORN

The pregnancy continued without any further problems. I was allowed to eat my beloved bread and crackers once again. All was well with the world.

At 39 weeks, I started having contractions. I continued to vomit through the labor, just like I did through the entire pregnancy.

After hours of labor with no progression, an emergency cesarean was performed when Mikayla's heartbeat dropped. The time from when the doctor told me we had to do a c-section until the baby was out was 14 minutes.

I knew as soon as my baby was out because I stopped vomiting, just like the labor and delivery nurse told me I would. With a blue curtain blocking my view, I couldn't see my baby. I knew babies were supposed to cry when they entered the world. But this baby made no sound. Was she breathing?

My heart and my breath waited for a sign of life. I yelled, "Is my baby okay?"

No one answered me. I yelled again and again. Craig held my hand in anticipation that she was okay.

It felt like an eternity to get an answer.

"Is my baby okay?"

Then my ears heard the wonderful sound of a baby's wail.

My baby crying out. My baby. A living, breathing, show-and-tell kind of baby.

"Look at what my God did!"

Psalm 106:1 — "Praise the LORD. Give thanks to the LORD, for he is good; for his love endures forever."

She was placed in Craig's arms, still screaming at the top of her lungs. Still on the table with my arms extended as if I were on a cross, he placed her next to my ear.

With tears in his eyes, he said, "Isn't she beaut-iful?"

I looked over at her for the first time and saw her little face. Without a filter in my mind, the words spilled out before I could take them back. "She looks like you!" I blurted out.

Craig laughed, thinking I was joking. Then he realized that I was serious. I had been dreaming about a little girl who looked like me, not him. If we'd had a boy, I would have been thrilled...but a baby girl?

All of the tension of an emergency c-section, all of the unknowns in the OR. All of the waiting to hear her cry. I'd been waiting for this miracle for years, and *that's* what came out of my mouth.

Geez.

She looked exactly like Craig. Spitting image. Craig's features were all wrapped up in a little swaddling blanket. This little girl looked like a man.

Thankfully, my little girl started to look more like a little girl within a few days and less like an old man. No one warned me about how babies look when they're first born.

In the maternity ward, an ultrasound was done on her heart. She had no heart defects at all. The hole had disappeared. Another miracle.

Craig held her, changed her, and rocked her to sleep. Meanwhile, I laid in the hospital bed recovering from the bubonic plague or chicken pox or the measles or something. Whatever it was, it was not fun. Turns out it was an allergic reaction to the epidural.

Just my luck.

Craig was a natural. I started to wonder if I would ever be as good as him at taking care of our baby. I only touched Mikayla when a nurse told me to. I felt detached.

Weren't my mothering skills just naturally supposed to kick in?

He asked if I wanted to hold her, and I said, "No, you keep doing what you're doing. You're so good at it."

What kind of mother doesn't want to hold her own baby? Maybe it's because of the reaction to the epidural?

Craig helped hold her while I adjusted, trying to nurse her. For the first time, her big blue eyes met mine. I gazed into her eyes as I held her in my arms. All I could think about was how I had missed seeing my four other babies' eyes.

What color would they be? Why, in the midst of celebration, could I only feel sadness, loss, and emptiness?

In true form, I kept all of these questions hidden away in the dark recesses of my heart. My own thoughts didn't make sense to me, so how was someone else supposed to understand them?

In an instant, the lie I had believed reared its ugly head. The reason I'd had so many miscarriages was because those babies knew I wouldn't be a good mother. There had been some kind of mistake; this baby made it somehow. If I touch her, I'm going to break her. I'm going to screw her up.

"No, Babe, you can hold her," I said again and again, afraid to speak what my heart felt. Such ugly matters of the heart stayed suppressed. Shame washed over me.

Jesus? Are you in this place? Are you here when I feel so unworthy of this baby? Are you here, right now? This moment? Will you teach me how to be a good mama? Will you show me how to love her like you do?

Psalm 77:2 — "When I was in distress, I sought the Lord; at night I stretched out untiring hands, and I would not be comforted."

On day three of being in the hospital, a co-worker came to visit. She started to change Mikayla's diaper. For the first time in three days, I actually desired to hold her, touch her, and cradle her. I wanted to tell the world she's mine.

"I'm going to be the best mother I can be," I wanted to shout from the rooftops.

I told my co-worker I hadn't changed my baby's diaper yet. With that one sentence, she stepped aside. I slowly made my way over to Mikayla Hope, who was lying in the bassinet. The fear of breaking her was gone. I cared for my little girl.

Hebrews 2:13a — ... "I will put my trust in Him."

My heart whispered, *you and I are going to make it. We're going to be just fine.*

My Mama's
Advice

The days and weeks following Mikayla's birth were filled with a peace and joy unlike any other. Motherhood suddenly clicked for me, as if I were born to be a mother. It was the first thing I had ever done in my life that felt so natural.

Those first few days in the hospital were not a preview of days to come, but just a moment of foreboding joy. Fear of losing my miracle baby caused me to guard my heart during that hospital stay.

But as we came home and settled into our new normal with a newborn baby, my guard melted away.

Psalm 30:11 — "You turned my wailing into dancing; you removed my sackcloth and clothed me with joy."

God truly answered my cries. Thanksgiving filled my heart. I was finally a mama. My arms were full. Craig's parents came to visit, and then my own parents flew to Los Angeles to meet their grandbaby, too.

In my parent's hotel room, I saw how much the MS was taking over my mama's body. A year earlier she could wrap her arms around me. But this time, my dad had to move her arms for her. It was the first time I had seen her so weak.

In the bed, her legs involuntarily curled up under her immobile body and froze in place under her torso. Her voice was almost a whisper now—a voice that at one time commanded an audience.

Her fingers, which used to type away at the computer keyboard with such force, were now just sticks of flesh and bone.

Her body was propped up by pillows to accommodate the weight of newborn Mikayla in her arms. Seeing her so frail made me realize how much she had to fight for joy.

Nehemiah 8:10b — "...for the joy of the LORD is your strength."

My mama would have missed the joy of holding her beloved prayer in flesh if her gaze had remained fixated on her own body, slowly fading in front of her.

Seeing her hold my little girl made me realize just how unrelenting she truly was. Her body was failing her from the dreadful disease, and yet she was here. With me. Holding my baby. She had begged God right along with me for a baby. How long she had prayed for this moment to happen!

She believed beyond human reason that a miracle baby would one day be in my arms. She encouraged me to believe that God would hear my cries.

My mama's strength in never ceasing to pray, her tenacity in faithfully seeking the Lord, and her faith in a loving God who desires good in our lives were reflected in how she trusted God to move mountains for me.

Psalm 31:24 — "Be strong and take heart, all you who hope in the LORD."

She had faith when I didn't. She prayed for me when I couldn't. She interceded for me when all I could do was hold onto the slightest bit of hope. A mama's prayers are powerful for the kingdom, and without those prayers, I don't know where I would be.

Holding our little miracle brought such delight to her eyes. She didn't miss the moment. My mama whispered to me, "Linni, please keep believing for more children. You were born to be a mother to many. Keep believing. Keep hoping."

TO MY BIGGEST CHEERLEADER

On a late summer evening, three weeks after my parents flew back home, I could not shake the feeling that I needed to call my parents. Mikayla was nine weeks old. I normally called every day to check in with them, but with the busyness of being a new mama, a few days slipped by without a short phone call home.

I called at midnight their time. It wasn't unusual for them to be up so late. I had just rocked Mikayla to sleep in our rocking chair. My dad picked up the phone. We chatted for two hours while he relayed my mom's words back to me. The phone could not pick up her inaudible speech.

We said our goodbyes with the promise to chat tomorrow. That was the longest conversation we'd had since they returned to Ohio.

The next morning, as I was stepping out of the shower, my phone rang.

"Hey, Linni," my brother choked out through raspy words and guttural sobs.

"What's wrong?" I begged, trying to piece together his words with water dripping from my wet hair.

"Haven't you heard the news? Didn't Dad call you?"

"No. What news?" I asked in a panic.

Hearing him sob on the phone, I could only make out the word "died." My mind raced, *Who could have died?* I instantly thought of our 85-year-old grandfather.

"Pap—Pap, died," I said more as an intended question, but it came out as a statement.

I started sobbing just as hard as my brother. I couldn't believe it. He was so healthy.

How could he have died?

I was supposed to call him later that day. I called him every Sunday, and now I would never make that phone call again.

My brother interrupted my thoughts and said, "No, Linni. Pap didn't die. Mom died."

"What?" I half-screamed, half-sobbed. "I just talked with her a few hours ago! She was totally fine!"

Shock and denial ran through my body like an uncontrollable wildfire.

Right in the midst of the wildfire, I had a picture of my mama dancing on the translucent streets of gold in Heaven, with her brown, curly hair in perfect form, just the way she'd always wanted her hair to look, with her long legs moving to the rhythm of a glorious song and the biggest smile on her face I had ever seen.

She was Home, dancing for the first time in decades. Peace quenched the wildfire of emotions within me. I knew it was her time to go.

Within seconds of hanging up the phone with my brother, I called my dad. Somehow, I had missed his phone call just before my brother's call.

He confirmed the news. Still in shock, we didn't have anything to say to each other but, "I love you."

The one person who believed in me most just left this earth.

I wrote this letter immediately after hearing the news and read it at my mom's funeral:

To My Mother,

The one who was always there for me, the one who was my biggest cheerleader, my biggest fan, and my biggest supporter—You, who always told me I could achieve anything if I put my mind to it. You were the one who told me to never give up, to never quit.

You were the ultimate example of what it meant to pick yourself up and try again. You never gave up, you never said quit. You persevered through your trials of everyday living. Of surviving. You saw life as one big adventure and refused to allow your circumstances to define who you were as a person, a mother, a wife.

You always had a smile on your face and always laughed about your ailing body. You never saw your trials as hardships, but embraced them to the best of your ability. I never saw you complain, but yet you were ready to go meet your Savior.

You wanted to see me get married and have children. You wanted to see your son marry his bride. You were able to see all of that before the Lord took you away.

You were a good mother—a great mother. The ultimate example of living for the Lord. You had a heart after the Lord's. You passed in your sleep this morning with a smile on your face. You finally got to meet Jesus, your Savior. I am at peace; I know you are Home.

Peace washed over me as I knew she wasn't suffering anymore, but little did I know how much of a loss I would feel with her gone. Little did I know what it would look like to hide hope in my heart with my biggest cheerleader no longer cheering me on.

Little did I know that with her death, my hope and faith in God would traverse the depths of human understanding.

Little did I know the rocky path I'd take, believing against all odds for another baby when I couldn't call my mama for reassurance.

"No, Linni, you're not crazy for believing the impossible," would never be said from her lips again.

Now, it was my turn to dig down deep and hold onto a faith that couldn't be explained while begging God for another miracle baby. With my mama's passing, I didn't know what a gift she gave me in her death. It would not be unwrapped for another year and a half.

SURPRISE!

It was Christmas. Mikayla Hope was 18 months old. Cinnamon, cloves, and nutmeg filled the air as the oven baked pies, cookies, and more holiday treats.

Our Christmas tree stood in the middle of our new living room in our new home, with white lights twinkling in the tree. I had just graduated summa cum laude from college. Celebration was in the air.

Our landlords called us while we were living in our one-bedroom apartment and asked if we would like to move into their three-bedroom house. All we had to do was name our price.

We named our price. They accepted our offer. Another miracle in Los Angeles. We were now living in a home with rent set at the same price as most one-bedroom apartments. Who couldn't see God's hand in that? Just another layer to our story of God moving mountains for us.

We tripled our square footage. With expanding our living space, the thought of expanding our family came to mind as well.

A few of my friends who were pregnant around the

same time as I was when I was pregnant with Mikayla were now pregnant with Baby Number Two.

> *Romans 8:28 — "And we know that in all things God works for the good of those who love him, who have been called according to his purpose."*

I was apprehensive about trying for another baby. Even if people were moving along in their lives by adding more children to their family, I wasn't sure about the timing or if my heart could handle another miscarriage.

Craig reminded me that our fertility specialist said he had fixed our problem. The septum that had caused the previous miscarriages was no longer in my uterus. We could have another baby and most likely have no complications. His confidence was contagious, but I still wanted to discuss and pray about it a little more.

Then, without warning, while we were still in the talking phase about getting pregnant, I started to put two and two together.

I have been sick an awful lot this week.

I took a pregnancy test, and within seconds, we had a double pink line.

"Babe, you won't believe this!" I shouted from the bathroom. He came running. I held up the pregnancy test. "We're pregnant."

He laughed and said, "Well, God has a funny way of answering us."

After four miscarriages and one full-term

pregnancy, we had a surprise. It was our sixth pregnancy!

It seemed fitting to be surprisingly pregnant at Christmas. After all, so many sermons on a Sunday morning in December are about Mary and Joseph and their travels to Bethlehem.

I'm sure Mary was surprised to hear that she would have to give birth where animals lay. Although I was surprised by this baby's arrival, I was pleasantly expecting good things to come our way.

James 1:17 — "Every good and perfect gift is from above, coming down from the Father of the heavenly lights, who does not change like shifting shadows."

After a quick calculation of a due date, I realized that this baby was most likely due a few days before the second anniversary of my mom's passing.

I told Craig, "If this baby is a girl, I want to name her Ellen, after my mama."

What a gift to give birth to a new life named in my mother's honor!

How Emotions Run Dry

In the early hours of dawn, I awoke to the bed sheets feeling damp beneath me. At first, I wondered if Mikayla had climbed into bed with a leaky diaper.

The bedroom was still dark, with a hint of the early morning sunlight starting to sneak past the blinds. I glanced down at my hand while I sat up on the side of the bed.

Blood. I'm covered in blood.

Job 17:1 — "My spirit is broken, my days are cut short, the grave awaits me."

I blinked a few times, staring at my damp hand, trying to gather my thoughts. I made my way to the bathroom and turned on the light switch. Right in front of my eyes, the toilet bowl was filled with blood and clumps of black tissue.

This can't be happening. We fixed the problem. The fertility specialist told me my chances of ever miscarrying again were slim to none.

Then my mind went blank with shock. Without even thinking or expressing any emotion, I silently retrieved a container from the kitchen and gathered the tissues from the toilet. I knew the doctor would want to do chromosomal testing.

I sat on the couch and stared into space, not wanting to wake Craig up too early in the morning.

While sitting on the couch, I lost track of time. I bled through my first pad and then another.

This is what hemorrhaging looks like, I thought with eerie calmness. *I've been warned of this.*

I tapped Craig on the shoulder, waking him from his sleep. "We need to go to the hospital," I said numbly.

In the ER, I lay on the hospital bed. The day became fuzzy. My mind was not engaged in the activities of the hospital. It was as if I were perched high above, looking down on myself, observing the comings and goings of the ER nurses and doctors into my room.

I sat in a daze, staring at my body down below, dressed in a white hospital gown and covered in stiff, white blankets.

I didn't say a single prayer that day, nor did I beg God to do anything. I accepted what I thought was my fate: to be an infertile mother of one.

It must have been a fluke for me to have one baby at home. How in the world did I carry one baby to term and not this one?

The faint, hazy memories of ultrasounds and IV bags and the constant barrage of questions from the hospital staff filled the day with such a blur. I laid on the bed, trying to watch a football game.

Anything to be normal for a minute. Just watch the game, Linni. Another unexplained miscarriage.

No reason for the sudden hemorrhaging was given.

I'm some kind of medical marvel.

It was the first time I had ever hemorrhaged during a miscarriage.

I need to be content. God only promised us one baby.

It's going to be okay, I convinced myself. *We'll be okay as a family of three. I just want to be home in my own bed right now.*

The desire to have more children was stuffed into the deep, dark recesses of my heart. A distant contentment took over.

The pain of another miscarriage was too great to bear. Instead of allowing myself to cry or feel broken, I turned off my emotions, just like a water faucet. My emotions ran dry. I consciously made a vow that no one would ever see me cry again. A steel superhero cape draped over my heart.

I did not shed a tear that day or the next or the next. I didn't shake my fist at God. I didn't shout or whisper any prayers. I just sat in the hollowness of having yet another unexplained miscarriage added to my medical chart.

COMPLICATED
LAYERS

My fifth miscarriage at 26 years of age brought me to my knees with a whole new level of pain I had never experienced before. The complicated layers of timing, grief, and pain were piled high.

When I shared with a friend that I had miscarried again, she whispered to me that she'd had an abortion when she was in college.

"Linni, the pain of your miscarriages mirrors mine about my abortion. I don't know why, but I understand what you're going through."

I was shocked to have her confide in me; and yet, somehow, in the deepest part of my heart, I understood where she was coming from, too.

This small conversation would be tucked away in my mind for a few more years before I could fully comprehend how her abortion and my miscarriages had the same root emotions of regret, sorrow, guilt, and pain.

I hugged her as she cried in my arms over her baby, gone too soon. Our pain connected us. I admired her ability to cry in front of me.

I called my dad to let him know that I miscarried. His new wife answered the phone. "I'll get your dad," she said.

"Hi, Honey!"

"Dad, I miscarried again." I told him, expecting to be comforted.

"Oh...I forgot you were pregnant," he admitted.

The pain I felt with his admission was severe.

How could he forget he had another grandbaby coming?

He had nothing else to say. I could sense his disconnection.

Psalms 27:10 — "Though my father and mother forsake me, the LORD will receive me."

I called another friend who was pregnant. She said, "Oh, I wish I would have miscarried and you hadn't," which translated in my heart as, *"I hate what you love."* More disconnection.

It would take me a few more years before I could gather up enough courage to let this person know that her words hurt me.

When I finally did have the courage to tell her, her response was one of the kindest reactions I could have asked for. She said with great sorrow, "Oh, Linni, please forgive me! I can't believe I said that!"

"Yes, of course, I never meant to hold it against you," I replied. "I never realized that I *did* hold it against you until recently. Please forgive me, too," I

responded, feeling my heart melt with her compassionate tone.

---

*Colossians 3:12 — "...clothe your--
selves with compassion, kindness,
humility, gentleness and patience."*

This miscarriage showed me how gracious I needed to be in response to others. I was stretched beyond
belief, learning how to have a kind response to those
who learned that I had miscarried again.

We tried to keep the news contained to just our
small circle of close friends, but unfortunately, word
spread quickly to the older church ladies.

While in my own pain, I had no idea how much
healing and forgiveness were required for others. Once
the church ladies found out I'd had my fifth
miscarriage, they responded with words of discourage-
ment, telling me to stop trying for a baby.

One lady admonished, "You need to focus on other
aspects of your life instead of having another child."

The complicated layers of grief over my mama and
my baby being gone made me sink into myself living
in a very quiet, lonely world, not know who to turn to
or who would understand.

THREE WEEPING WILLOW TREES

Growing up, I had three huge weeping willow trees in my backyard that towered over the far end of our property line.

Weeping willows are called such because the branches bend downward, resembling a large umbrella. Heavy in weeping, their branches can touch the ground. The trees are planted to take what is swampy, unusable land and turn it into dry, usable ground. The willows soak up all of the wet soil with their deep roots.

The tree trunks are strong, but the branches are brittle. They are tall, and yet the branches bend down to the soil.

I looked strong and capable, yet one ill word spoken could snap a branch in all the wrong places of my being.

My baby. Gone. The dream of growing our family. Gone. Fullness of life. Gone.

My heart secretly wept, but my tears were stored away in the hollowness of my being. I tried to rationalize my grief, pushing away my emotions that

I could no longer understand or try to explain.

I was the weeping willow tree. Hollow and empty. Brittle and frail, bent over from secretly weeping.

I had one baby in my arms.

Why can't I be happy? Why can't I just be content, like so many women in our little church keep telling me to be?

I was told that God's sovereignty allowed this baby to go. That it wasn't God's timing for this one to make it into this world.

Such words are meant for a theological classroom debate, but not for the heart of a bereaved mama-to-be. Well-meaning words of comfort twisted in this mama's ears and heart to sound as if she was wrong for grieving, for weeping for her unborn child, for questioning God's purpose for her life.

Alone in my living room, I pushed "play" for a song to be sung aloud. My limbs rose above my head, swaying to the beat of the drum. With my eyes closed and my legs firmly planted on solid ground, I sang the sorrowful words of King David's Psalm.

"Oh why, God? Why? Where are you, God? Have you forgotten me?"

There, the Lord took me deeper. There, I recognized it for what it was: natural grief.

My "aha" moment of a lifetime.

My sorrow for my own mama gone was the same sorrow of my own baby, too.

There. My mama's gift to me.

How special to recognize that this grieving heart was not questioning God as if He were wrong but only longing to be embraced in her Heavenly Father's arms.

If grieving for my mama was okay, then crying over my baby was, too.

What a gift of freedom I found in my own mama's death! Loss is loss, no matter how it occurs.

Death is death, no matter how long the life is sustained. Grief is natural, even godly. The shortest verse in the Bible says it all: "Jesus wept."

Ah, the freedom to no longer wrestle with my tears, but to let them flow, just as the weeping willow tree allows her limbs to bend low.

There in song and dance, I found freedom to weep in front of my King. I, no longer ashamed of hidden emotions I could not explain, knew what these tears were now. They were tears made of salt and water, made to clean festering wounds and heal this weeping daughter.

In the privacy of my home, strength came from these tears that fell to the ground. My roots drank the living water, hoping this tree would no longer be bound.

Number Two

The following summer, Mikayla Hope turned two years old. It was as if the number two was a magical number that automatically signaled to the outside world that one child was not enough.

The questions and comments were coming from every angle. Even the church ladies who told us to stop trying for Baby Number Two were now telling us to have another. It was disorienting to receive such conflicting advice.

"When are you going to have Baby Number Two?"

"She's two now; she needs a sibling."

"You guys are such good parents. We can't imagine you with only one child."

"Well, don't wait forever, this is how God blesses you."

It felt like all of the pain of our lost babies, the ones who never made it into our arms, was forgotten. Life moved on for them, but I was still secretly mourning.

Life stood still for me. These questions and comments felt condemning to me. After all, how many years did it take us to get pregnant with Mikayla?

How many times had we tried for a baby? I knew this was not in my control.

My responses were less than stellar most of the time. I am not proud of my reaction to these questions. I even posted on social media, "The next person who asks me if we're going to have another baby, I'm going to say "#$@!&% shut up" and then I'm going to turn my back and walk away." A woman who was also struggling with losing her baby commented, "Thank you. I feel the same."

At one point, in response to, "When are you going to have Baby Number Two?" I angrily bit back with heated breath, "Oh, you mean Baby Number Seven?" in such a sarcastic manner that I instantly regretted even opening my mouth when I saw my friend's eyes widen with hurt and shock.

Oh, how I hurt those who never intended to hurt me. I miscarried friendships by squeezing the throats of beloved friends while my own heart was still broken. I had no idea how to respond with grace and kindness in the midst of pain.

My anger came from wanting so badly to understand why this was happening, knowing full well I may never know the answer.

I realized I only knew two things:

1) God still loves me.
2) I don't understand any of this.

It felt like an unbalanced seesaw in my heart. On one side, I knew that God sees me, cares for me, and loves me. On the other side, I knew heartache, disappointment, and disillusionment.

Would God ever take any of the achings in my heart away?

The pain lessened as I learned to be still in His presence. To accept His mystery. To accept that I wasn't owed an explanation was a new holy surrender. The months after our last miscarriage seemed to heal the acute pain, but would there ever be a life of abundance and true joy again? It seemed unfathomable.

AIN'T NO ONE GONNA BELIEVE THIS!

While pushing a stroller in the middle of the Los Angeles Zoo on a sweltering late summer day, I received a friend's text message: "I'm praying for you to have a baby."

I looked at my phone and laughed to myself—*I don't know about that.*

Craig had just given his two-week notice. We were downsizing to one income as he was planning to stay home with Mikayla while starting a new career. We knew it would take awhile for his new career to take off and be profitable. So, we were taking another leap of faith with this decision.

I don't know if I want another baby right now!

Fear ran through my mind while rereading her text message.

I don't want to miscarry again.

What happened next will always and forever be branded on my heart. My mind. My soul. I've never experienced something so profound. So crazy. So beautiful. So strange. So wonderful. So hard to explain.

In the middle of the walkway to the gorilla habitat,

I froze in mid-stride. I heard a voice that completely interrupted my fearful thoughts.

It was a never-heard-God's-audible-voice-before-or-since kind of moment.

"Her name will be Victoria Faith," the Voice whispered audibly in my ear.

I quickly glanced over my shoulder with wild eyes full of faith.

Did anyone else hear what I just heard?

This name, "Victoria Faith," was spoken clearly, audibly. I couldn't deny it. Craig and I had never discussed this name. I never daydreamed of such a name. This name came from the Lord.

I, the same woman who was told she had a ten percent chance of ever having children, was just given the name of her second miracle baby while pushing her first miracle baby in a stroller at the zoo, of all places.

Victoria Faith is coming.

God speaks to accomplish. My heart leapt with joy.

Isaiah 55:11 — "[S]o is my word that goes out from my mouth: It will not return to me empty, but will accomplish what I desire and achieve the purpose for which I sent it."

I knew it in my spirit and my soul. I knew it in my being, my heart, and my head.

Victoria Faith is our daughter's name.

I decided to wait until Craig returned home from

work to share the news of our promised baby.

I was no longer scared to get pregnant again. I was no longer scared to miscarry. I had a new vision for my life and our family: two little girls running around our house soon. The dream of more children could finally come true!

Throughout the day, my mind was filled with to-do lists, cleaning, and toddler activities galore. Somehow, the promised name slipped my mind.

Eventually, around 10:00 p.m., Craig walked through the door. I looked up from my book while I reclined on the couch. "Hi, Babe. How was your day?" I asked.

To which he responded, "I'm exhausted. I'm going to bed."

Throughout our marriage, I've always been the morning lark, and he, the night owl. For the first time in our lives, he was going to bed before me.

I closed my book and stared at him as if he were some kind of alien that had abducted my husband. "What? You can't go to bed!" I protested with a shout.

"Why not?" he replied, perturbed that I was telling him what to do.

My stomach turned in knots. I had no answer for him.

Why wasn't he allowed to go to bed yet?

My mind couldn't answer, but a knowing from my heart came out of my mouth. "You have something you're supposed to tell me," I said. "The Lord is telling me you have something to say."

"I have no idea what that would be," he replied, his eyes wild with annoyance and his tired shoulders hunched over from a long day. He only had a few days left of work and was trying to get everything in order for his replacement.

Then, suddenly, he popped up from his stupor. "Aha! I know it! I know what it is!"

"Really, what?" I asked, more confused about that than why he couldn't go to bed and had to stay awake.

'The Lord told me the name of our next baby! Her name will be Victoria Faith!"

Now it was my turn to be shocked.

Didn't the Lord tell me that yesterday?

"What?!" I exclaimed as I ran to him. "The Lord told me that yesterday. Wait! No, He told me that today!"

My sentences rushed by so fast that he asked me to repeat my words. They spilled out of my soul and out of my mouth. "God told me the same name!" I cried.

There we were, in the living room of our beloved three-bedroom home, ready for it to be filled with another little one to call our own. We jumped up and down rejoicing together. "Victoria Faith is coming! She's coming," we cried with praise overflowing from our mouths.

We stopped jumping up and down. I looked up at Craig. With our arms still around each other, he looked down at me. "Ain't no one gonna believe this!" he exclaimed.

The excitement permeated every fiber of our beings. New life and new hope came to rest in our home.

TIGHTROPES

In early fall, a month after our crazy-super-cool encounter with God, we found out we were pregnant! As soon as the double line appeared on the pregnancy test, we knew Victoria Faith was coming.

I called my doctor and asked for a pregnancy (HCG) blood test. I knew not to delay getting an ultrasound. Waiting another month for an eight-week ultrasound would be torture for me.

The excitement that God just spoke, and then, the following month, that I was pregnant, was overwhelmingly incredible.

Years earlier, when God said that we would have a baby, we had to wait two years before Mikayla Hope came. This time, we'd only waited a few weeks. Joy was in the air. Life was ready to come forth.

A few days later, I walked into the doctor's office. An older nurse, Gizel from Croatia, drew my blood. She was the same nurse I'd had when I was pregnant with Mikayla. She remembered my name, and I remembered hers. We had a strong bond.

Her grandmotherly touch always blessed me. She

was the kind of woman who made me feel like I was the only patient she would have that day. She had all the time in the world for me.

She ran to hug me when I walked through the door. "Why are you here, sweetheart? Everything okay?" she asked.

"Everything's fine, I'm pregnant!" I said with a squeal, hugging her back.

I sat down for the blood to be drawn and told her how I was getting nervous that I might miscarry. Yet, I was ready to be a mama again. The tension between peace and anxiety walked a fine line, like walking on a tightrope in my heart.

"Oh, honey, you'll be fine! Trust me!" She consoled me with a pat on my hand.

I walked back to my car with the peace of knowing that Jesus was with me.

1 Peter 5:7 — "Cast all your anxiety on him because he cares for you."

The following afternoon, while at work, I received the call from the doctor's office that I had been waiting for.

"Linni, your bloodwork came back." Her tone did not sound good.

Oh no, please no...

"Your HCG levels are in the lower range, based on the dates that you gave us. We want you to come back in for more bloodwork."

"So, I haven't miscarried yet?" I asked, trying to

hold on to hope.

"Correct, you're still pregnant, but your levels are not as high as I think they should be. Maybe the conception date is wrong."

I breathed a sigh of relief, *Oh, thank God! I'm still pregnant.*

DUTY FIRST

I slowly made my way up the stairs of the high school where I worked. My mind was cloudy and foggy from the highs and lows of the emotional roller coaster while playing the waiting game on my bloodwork results.

A crowd of teenagers pushed past me to get to class. I willed my feet to take the next step.

Would this baby survive in my womb? I wondered to myself as the swarm of teenagers grew and kept pushing past me on the stairs.

Of course I'm still pregnant; God gave us the promise that Victoria Faith is coming.

The odds of both Craig and I hearing the same first and middle names were insane. We knew we had a promised child on the way. But little did we know how excruciating the wait would be.

As my foot hit the last step of the stairs, I felt a drip of blood. Then another. Then, to my utter disbelief, I felt tissue come out of me.

I walked faster to the bathroom, knowing I'd be late to class. I prayed under my breath that maybe my mind was just playing tricks on me and maybe it wasn't blood or tissue after all.

As I entered the bathroom stall, my eyes confirmed what my mind was trying to rationalize. I was miscarrying. Blood and black tissue filled the toilet. I was too stunned to cry. Anger rushed over my entire body.

Didn't you just promise us a baby? Now this baby is gone, too? I silently screamed at God.

I quickly cleaned myself up and briskly walked to my class around the corner.

Put on a brave face, Linni. Everything is going to be fine. Maybe I'm not miscarrying; maybe I'm just spotting, I told myself, even though I knew with that amount of blood I couldn't just be spotting.

Job 17:15 — "[W]here then is my hope—who can see any hope for me?"

I made my way to my next class and sat in my interpreting chair, ready to interpret, when the denial faded and reality hit me. A miscarriage was indeed happening.

I choked back tears as I stood up to tell my colleague that I needed to call a sub.

Oh my god, I really am losing my baby.

He asked me what was wrong as I rushed out the door. Without warning, tears spilled over and onto my cheeks. "I'm miscarrying," I blurted out without thinking, embarrassed that I could not stop the tears from flowing, wiping them away as fast as they came.

I was even more embarrassed that I had just told a man that I was miscarrying, exposing a vulnerable part of my heart.

Within an hour, my doctor had me sitting in his exam room. The bloodwork results from the day before weren't back yet. I sat erect in a wooden chair, waiting for him to come in. The nurse didn't even have me sit on the exam table. I should have known then that there was no point to this visit.

He and his nurse came into the room. He calmly explained, "There is no reason for doing an ultrasound because you are so early in this pregnancy. There isn't anything to see, especially since you have already passed the tissue."

My entire body, engulfed in flames of anger, blew up. "You will do an ultrasound, and you will find a heartbeat!" I barked, even though I knew a heartbeat couldn't be detected yet. "Please, do something!" I begged.

My doctor grabbed my hand and said, "I'm so sorry."

I forced the tears that were threatening to emerge back into the deep recesses of my heart.

> *Psalm 102:1 — "Hear my prayer,*
> *LORD; let my cry for help come to*
> *you."*

"We need to wait on that bloodwork before we do anything. Your previous levels won't show us anything on the ultrasound," he said.

I took a deep breath and straightened myself up like a brick wall around the city of Jericho.

I've been through miscarriages before. I know how to handle this.

A "duty first" mentality took over. I drove back to work, faked a smile, and held in all of my emotions. It was all I could do.

But inside, I was a million pieces of broken glass, shattered and disillusioned with the medical community *and* with God.

I didn't even realize until a few hours later that I hadn't called Craig to let him know that I drove to the hospital or that I went back to work. I didn't want to say any words out loud. That would make it real.

Psalm 42:6a — "My soul is downcast within me..."

I didn't want anyone to take care of me. There was nothing anyone could do. Weeks ago, Craig and I rejoiced over new life. We were one. But now I swam back to my own deserted island, built for one, bearing all of the pain seemingly alone.

DÉJÀ VU

Survival and self-preservation took over. Craig had no clue how to comfort me. I didn't expect him to comfort me any longer.

I convinced myself that I needed to just focus on the daughter in my arms and not on the pain of another baby who wasn't in my arms. I knew we were promised Victoria Faith, but "when" and "how" were two mysteries hanging over my head.

We decided to go back to our Reproductive Endocrinologist (RE) to see if tests could be run to figure out why I kept miscarrying, especially after the surgery he performed.

Craig and I walked into the doctor's beautifully decorated office, complete with crystal chandeliers and marble top coffee tables, as if it had been frozen in time since our last visit three years before. I knew it was going to be an expensive detour on our path to Victoria Faith. It was a leap of faith to believe we could even afford this appointment.

The doctor remembered us. His face lit up the moment he saw me. He welcomed us into his back office with open arms. He hugged me tightly. I knew we were with the right doctor yet again.

He asked to see pictures of our daughter. We jumped at the chance to show her off—a miracle baby that he had a hand in. We hoped he would be able to pull off another miracle, just like before.

He did an ultrasound to see if he could find the reason we continued to miscarry after Mikayla. It was possible that maybe the septum had not been fully removed or the embryos were not implanting in the correct spot.

There on the exam table, with my legs in the all-too-familiar cold stirrups, he turned on the machine. With a flip of a switch, the machine came to life. The machine I started referring to as a torture device. The machine I nicknamed, "The Beast of Truth." The black screen became bright in the darkened room. My uterus was on full display.

The doctor said, "Linni, your uterus is as beautiful as ever. There is nothing wrong at all. A small part of the septum is still there, but it shouldn't be an issue. Just to make sure, let's do bloodwork and see if it's your hormones."

I got dressed and looked at Craig. "Let's do this," I said with a new resolve, a confident smile spread across my face. We both had hope that this would give us answers.

We walked down the hall to the room where the blood was drawn. The technician remembered us. She was overjoyed to see us in the office! She gushed, "How is your baby!?"

I told her Mikayla was a bright, blue-eyed little

girl with the most beautiful white-blonde hair you have ever seen.

We drove home through the LA traffic. By the time we arrived, the doctor's office called us with the results of the bloodwork, since they did everything in-house. This was the benefit of seeing a RE.

"Your bloodwork came back completely normal. You are within the *normal* ranges for absolutely every test we ran on you."

I had never been so completely devastated to be told that I was "normal" in my life. To hear that there was nothing wrong also meant that there was nothing to fix.

How could a healthy 27-year-old have seven pregnancies and six miscarriages?

It was déjà vu all over again.

After a few more visits and even more bloodwork, the doctor put his hand to his forehead. Shoulders hunched over, looking at my chart, he empathetically said, "Secondary Unexplained Infertility is my diagnosis for you. I thought I fixed this."

There was something about his body language, his deflated demeanor, his perplexed expression over my tests that caused faith to stir in me. I started to giggle uncontrollably, making the label of Secondary Unexplained Infertility bounce right off me.

After all the years of wanting a doctor to see me—truly see me—here was this doctor doing just that. He was devastated for me at his own diagnosis. Oh, the irony!

My doctor and I switched emotional roles. I couldn't keep my laughter to myself. I tried to comfort him, "Only God can fix me! You've done your best."

With that diagnosis, it would be the last time we visited his office. I knew that if Victoria Faith was coming, it would be a true miracle from God.

Even still, I yearned to be in the Lord's presence day and night. I knew this emotional roller coaster all too well, and I didn't want to drown in the relentless darkness as I had in years past.

Isaiah 30:21 — "Whether you turn to the right or to the left, your ears will hear a voice behind you, saying, 'This is the way, walk in it.'"

In His presence was the only place on Earth where I felt His light of hope shine on me. To stave off the looming oppression, I would grab a blanket. Turn on the worship music. Lie on the floor. Let Heaven wash over me. Just. To. Survive.

SOAKING

Lying on my living room floor, I started to ascend a spiritual ladder to greater intimacy with the Lord. The longer I laid still, the more my festering wounds of the past healed. It was in my stillness where Jesus was renewing me.

I no longer wanted a safe religion, where life was predictable—having a house with a white picket fence, two and one-half kids, and a dog. I desired a life where I didn't always know where God's voice would take me. Where Mikayla Hope would grow up knowing she was a miracle and that God would continue to do miracles in her life.

The God of the Bible didn't ask anyone to play it safe. And He wasn't asking me to play it safe, either. He was asking me to believe against all odds that we would have another child.

God asked Abraham and Sarah to move to an unknown land and believe He would give them a child. He joined Shadrach, Meshach, and Abednego to walk in the fiery furnace. He anointed John the Baptist to lead the way in the wilderness.

He empowered Stephen to be a voice speaking the truth of Jesus Christ as Savior.

I wanted a life that mirrored the Old Testament prophets and the New Testament believers.

My faith felt too big to be put into a check box on a daily planner to appease the church ladies every time they asked if I was reading my Bible and doing my devotionals. I never felt like God was requiring me to read my Bible—I desired to read it!

I wanted to see more miracles, like what I read about! My hope was rising on that living room floor; anxiety lessened, and the grip of death loosened its hold on me.

This place was where His steadfast faithfulness was tangible day and night. Where peace surpassed all understanding from sunrise to sunset. Where hope and trust were birthed in greater measure in the midst of uncertainty. Where the church ladies' opinions no longer carried the weight they once did. Where only the Lord's opinion was the one that mattered.

Psalm 27:4 — "One thing I ask from the LORD, this only do I seek: that I may dwell in the house of the LORD all the days of my life, to gaze on the beauty of the LORD and to seek him in his temple."

The months went by and I continued to soak in the Lord's presence, seeking His face. Crying out for God to make Craig and me a living testimony: declaring that He still speaks and fulfills His promises today.

Craig and I did not try to prevent pregnancy, but I no longer obsessively shaded the ovulation days on the calendar, either.

The promise of Victoria Faith was at the forefront of my mind. It was the hope that kept me alive. Many nights, as I would fall asleep, I saw Victoria Faith in my dreams. God was not letting me forget that He likes to fulfill His promises.

MOUNTAIN-TOP ENCOUNTER

After ten months of Craig working on getting his career off the ground, and of lying prostrate on the floor before the Lord and seeing every single bill paid, I could sense a shift in my heart.

We had no background that gave us labels or even an understanding of what He was asking us to do. We were in our own spiritual no-man's land, walking by faith and not by sight, blazing our own path with the Lord.

We had no other present-day stories to model. We only had the Word of God. We had the story of the Israelites wandering in the wilderness as God provided manna for them each day. We had the story of Joseph feeding an entire nation. We had the stories of Jesus multiplying bread and fish. Those were the stories that we kept at the forefront of our minds.

We came together as a couple. We were ascending the ladder together. We were learning how to lean on each other in uncertainty. Not with infertility, yet—that would come many years later—but with life in general.

Craig awoke one morning knowing that he needed to hike up a mountain in Griffith Park. We nicknamed it, "Mount Sinai."

This was a mountain we hiked together many times over in the last ten months as I was processing Craig's job change and the loss of my mama and our babies.

Hiking together became a form of therapy. Sweating out all of the disappointments life had thrown at us and carrying all of the dreams we held in the deep recesses of our hearts uphill together made the load seem lighter.

This particular morning, Craig said, "I need to climb this mountain alone."

What? Without me? Seriously?

I was miffed. But in my heart, I knew he needed to go alone.

As Craig drove away, I prayed that the Holy Spirit would allow me to experience the moment he ascended to the top.

Sure enough, a few hours later, the sweet presence of the Holy Spirit filled our living room. This was the first time I had ever experienced a supernatural encounter with the Holy Spirit like this. A cloud filled our living room.

This was beyond my earthly understanding, but I knew in every fiber of my being it was the Lord. I looked at my precious little Mikayla Hope and proclaimed beyond a shadow of a doubt, "We are standing on holy ground." I felt like Moses in the wilderness standing before the burning bush.

I fell on my face before the Lord and cried, "We are

willing to do whatever you ask, Lord."

I knew right then and there that when Craig came home to tell me of his own encounter with the Lord, we were to do whatever God told him to do.

A few hours later, when he arrived back home, he was glowing. Literally. The kind of glow that was written about Moses after being in the presence of God in Exodus 34. Craig's face was the modern-day equivalent of this Old Testament encounter.

> *Exodus 34:29 — "When Moses came down from Mount Sinai... he was not aware that his face was radiant because he had spoken with the LORD."*

He said, "Well, I am not supposed to get another job yet."

"I know that. That is not earth-shattering enough. What else are we supposed to do?"

Shocked that I was onboard with that, he cautiously continued, "Well...we are supposed to pack up our house."

I screamed, "I knew it! The Lord told me last week, *'Out with the old and in with the new!'* I've been sorting our things for a week! I have one room left to organize!"

MULTIPLICATION

We started packing, not knowing where we were going or what we were doing. We were a living Old Testament Abraham and Sarah, just much, much younger.

The summer was approaching, and my next paycheck wouldn't come for two more months. This act of obedience seemed radical beyond our own understanding.

We rented a tiny storage unit. We put our bedroom furniture and our kitchen items in it. We gave away the majority of our other belongings, including my beloved rocking chair.

The recipient was a woman who desperately desired a miracle of her own. It was time to pass along my altar to the Lord, representing a promise, to the next person who needed a daily reminder that God is faithful to fulfill His promises.

Moving without a plan really couldn't be explained to anyone. We felt crazy to make such a ludicrous decision. We kept it to ourselves while we packed. Once we loaded our last box into the storage unit, we finally told our small group about Craig's encounter on the mountain five weeks earlier.

We tried to explain as best we could that we packed without knowing what the future held, but that we knew the Lord was in it. To our amazement, they gave us $100.00.

It looked like God was answering my prayer of not wanting a normal, boring life. My hope was high that we would continue to experience miracles.

We drove 18 hours straight through the night. In the morning, we arrived at Craig's parents' house in Colorado with only the clothes in our car. We had no plan to return to Los Angeles anytime soon.

We assumed this was a good place to land for a bit while we figured out what in the world God was doing. Following God doesn't always make sense. We were convinced we were the most insane people we had ever met! We were believing for a baby and for Craig's career to take off, which seemed to be taking a lot longer than we thought it would.

We arrived with $3.00 in our pockets and not another dime to our name. God had multiplied our gas on the way there. We had driven to Colorado six months earlier at Christmas time, and we paid $300.00 for gas. This time we only paid $97.00. Little did we know that Craig's aunt and uncle had been praying that God would multiply our gas for us, and that they had been recounting the stories to each other of when God had multiplied their gas.

After experiencing a New Testament miracle of multiplication, the Bible became more real with each supernatural miracle we witnessed that summer.

The promise of another child, Victoria Faith, was very present in my mind. Secondary Unexplained Infertility would not be my future. I knew one day she would come.

If the same Voice that told both of us her name while Craig and I were apart was also the same Voice that told us to pack our house while we were apart, then both words were true, and she was indeed coming.

During this time of being in Colorado, sleeping on my in-laws' floor, I started to see our future daughter's name, Victoria Faith, as not just a promise for her life, but God's promise of His character in our lives.

I clung to who God is. He is victoriously faithful. He is a God who brings forth life, not death. He is a God who provides solace in the midst of chaos. He is the God who calms the storm. He is the God who loves to show off and create miracles for his own glory. He is the God who laid with me on the floor.

There were too many unknowns to count. Staying in Colorado, without a penny to our names, we became completely reliant on the food my in-laws provided.

> *2 Corinthians 9:10 — "Now he who supplies seed to the sower and bread for food will also supply and increase your store of seed and will enlarge the harvest of your righteousness."*

However, the amount of food in my in-laws' fridge wasn't going down. My mother-in-law only went to the grocery store a couple of times during our six-week stay.

The same casserole had been sitting on the refrigerator shelf for days and days. Each time, I would dish out a slice for my family members and put the casserole dish back in the fridge. To my astonishment, the next day the casserole looked as though only one slice had been taken out of it. The following day, the same thing happened. God was multiplying our food before our very eyes.

Mark 16:17a — "And these signs will accompany those who believe..."

ETERNITY

Shortly after arriving in Colorado, I wasn't feeling well at all. It was the familiar feeling of intense nausea. Dread hit me. I did not want to be pregnant under these circumstances of not knowing where we were going to live and I certainly didn't want to miscarry the promise of Victoria Faith if I was actually pregnant.

I drove to the store. I charged a pregnancy test to our credit card. I took the test in the bathroom at Target. Sure enough, I was pregnant.

The paralysis of fear enveloped my entire body. The fear of miscarrying—the fear of being pregnant while homeless—the fear of not being able to provide for this baby—the fear of losing this miracle yet again.

I drove back to Craig and whispered to him that we needed to take a walk. I told him my secret once we were outside, facing the Colorado Rocky Mountains. "I'm pregnant."

He was overjoyed with the news, and I sighed a deep sigh of relief.

This baby is coming.

This was our sign that the God who is Victoriously Faithful is truly at work in our story—a story of giving up our house to follow Him on this wild goose chase.

We made the decision not to tell anyone about this coming baby. It was too painful to explain to ourselves, let alone to anyone else, that we were adding another mouth to feed in our circumstances.

Please, God, let us keep this baby.

Every moment that anxiety tempted its way into my mind, I would stop and visualize myself kicking it out.

I replace it with the peace of God.

Hebrews 11:6 — "And without faith it is impossible to please God, because anyone who comes to him must believe that he exists and that he rewards those who earnestly seek him."

I kept standing on God's promise that Victoria Faith was coming, staving away the looming storm in my heart.

A few days later, in the early hours of dawn, I arose from my makeshift bed on the floor of my in-laws' living room to use the restroom. As I did, I could feel blood dripping between my legs as my abdomen started twisting in pain. My heart sank into my stomach. My mouth became dry. My body glistened with sweat.

I sat on the toilet and caught my tiny baby in my

hands. I could feel my baby's curved spine. It felt so cruel to flush this little one down the toilet. Yet, there were no other options. No funeral. No memorial service. Nothing to show that there was a life needing to be remembered.

At 28 years old, this baby was my seventh miscarriage. I made the decision not to go to the hospital. I knew that there was nothing the doctors could do for me anyway, except inflict more trauma on an already traumatized soul. I couldn't have cared less about the RhoGAM shot for my blood type.

I resolved that I would not go into despair. I would not let this break me. I would stand strong. I rationalized that God was victoriously faithful, and this baby must not have been Victoria Faith.

I informed my husband that we had lost our baby. He was stoic, not knowing how to comfort me. I had no emotions. I was numb to this familiar pain.

That evening, I walked around my in-laws' neighborhood block. I looked towards the Rocky Mountains. The deep, orange sunset streaked across the sky. The mountains were majestically purple in all their glory.

I pleaded for God to speak. To explain why this would happen yet again. To calm the storm in my heart. And with that plea, the Creator of the World answered my heart's cry.

In an instant, I was taken up into what I would later call a vision, similar to the Apostle Paul saying he was caught up into the Third Heaven from 2 Corinthians 2.

I was no longer walking on the sidewalk in

Colorado, but on the translucent streets of gold in Heaven. These streets were the same golden streets that I saw the day my mom passed away.

At that moment, I saw Eternity.

As I stepped onto the golden pavement, I looked up towards a bright, white light. It transformed into the most gorgeous sunset I have ever seen, even more magnificent than any Colorado evening sky.

The Lord spoke to my heart, *"Linni, if you only knew what eternity was like, you would not question my goodness. People need to hear your testimony of My faithfulness. I will never leave you nor forsake you."*

In an instant, I was back on the sidewalk of Colorado, trying to get my bearings. My mourning over this baby was supernaturally lifted from my body. The despair was replaced with a joy that is not of this earth. Psalm 30:11 became real to me. God turned my mourning into dancing. It was true. The pain of losing my baby instantly vanished.

Psalm 30:11 — "You turned my wailing into dancing; you removed my sackcloth and clothed me with joy."

I walked back to my in-laws' house as if I was a New Testament Believer. I'd just had an encounter with the Creator of Heaven and Earth. I finally had purpose in my pain that had turned into dancing. People needed to know that God cares about their deepest anguish. That He can heal the ugliest of scars and gangrene wounds.

FAITH

A few weeks later, we drove back to Los Angeles with a faith that did not falter. Craig's aunt and uncle gave us money to stay at a couple of hotels and buy food on our way back to California.

We did not have plans beyond our arrival in California. It would be four more weeks until I received my next paycheck from the school. We were walking by faith and not by sight.

On the final leg of our journey, I awoke just east of Las Vegas not knowing where we would spend the night or what we would eat. We had $25 left until my next paycheck.

I awoke with such peace in my spirit, knowing that God was going to take care of us. Since my encounter, I didn't have a worry in the world about anything. The worst-case scenario: we would sleep on the beach that night.

That's not so bad!

Still lying in bed, I turned my head to see a text on my phone: "Hey! Are you guys back in town yet? If so, would you want to come over for dinner? If you don't have a place to stay, you can sleep at our house!" It was the same friend who had said she wished she had miscarried and not me. The redemption in this act of kindness was deeply felt.

And with that, we knew exactly where we were staying and that we would have dinner waiting for us! Our hope was on full display for all to see.

We stayed at their house for a few days. Then another family offered to have us stay at their house next! The plan was to stay with them for a couple of days, but we were having such a grand time telling them about all the miracles of multiplication we had experienced, they ended up inviting us to stay at their house for an entire week.

This family was living on food stamps. Here we were, dining at their home as if we were kings and queens. Their "yes" to our staying with them was a beautiful sacrifice. The connection was healing.

Romans 12:8 a—a "[I]f it is to
encourage, then give encouragement;
if it is giving, then give generously; if
it is to lead, do it diligently; if it is to
show mercy, do it cheerfully."

At the end of our stay, another family offered to have us live with them in their guest room. So, for the next nine weeks, we lived there while trying to get back on our feet. They loved on us and gave us space to process all that had happened in the last year without judgment.

It felt like every time we started saving money for a deposit on an apartment, our car broke down. We were being sifted like wheat. Could we really hold onto hope that the God of miracles would do another miracle for us?

At the end of nine weeks, lo and behold, another family offered to let us stay in their pop-up camper that was parked in their side yard. We were ecstatic to have another temporary resting place.

I told them, "I think we will only be here for a month, enough time for us to save for a deposit on an apartment."

THE CAMPER

We ended up living in that canvas pop-up camper on the good graces of our friends for 18 months. It was the most difficult 18 months of my life.

I silently cried myself to sleep many nights, as the camper was the same temperature outside as it was inside. I never wanted Craig to feel bad for his family living in such conditions. I hid my tears.

Psalm 23:4 — "Even though I walk through the darkest valley, I will fear no evil, for you are with me; your rod and staff, they comfort me."

Craig slept on the queen mattress that popped out, with our three-year-old Mikayla Hope sleeping next to him. We had the space heater facing her to keep her warm. I slept on the table converted into a tiny twin-ish bed.

We slept with fleece beanies on our heads, covering our ears, and many layers covering our bodies trying to stay warm in the winter.

During the summer, we could barely breathe inside the camper. The hot sun seemed tortuous as it blazed down on us, making the camper a human-sized oven.

Even if we were renting this camper for a small fee from our friends, I knew we were one step away from homelessness. We couldn't afford to rent the camper and save for a deposit on a future apartment. It was an endless cycle of poverty—one we had never experienced before.

I had no idea why we were there or what God was doing, but I knew we had to hold tightly to the hope of Jesus Christ.

Romans 8:28 — "And we know that in all things God works for the good of those who love him, who have been called according to his purpose."

Most nights, I would lay on my twin-table camper bed begging the Lord for an answer as to when Victoria Faith would come. I believed that if she came, then we wouldn't be homeless anymore. Jesus would get the glory for delivering us out of the camper and putting another baby in our arms.

After 11 months of living there, our friends who owned the camper said, "We would be okay if you were pregnant while living in the camper."

"What!?" I asked. "Where did that come from?"

"Oh, well, my husband had a dream that you were

pregnant. If you do become pregnant, you're welcome to continue living with us," the wife said.

I was shocked that someone had a dream of my being pregnant.

Especially since being intimate with my husband in a place where privacy was few and far between seemed to be a small feat.

I was even more shocked that they would be okay with us still living with them longer than we already had. We felt like we were running out of grace. I was done with living in a camper, but all other options of living in an apartment seemed to be dead ends.

In the meantime, Mikayla turned four years old over the summer.

She kept praying the cutest little prayer, "Jesus, baby sistah, peeze!" each night.

Her heart's desire for a baby sister echoed my own desire for that baby, spoken of in a promise two years prior.

A few weeks after the conversation with our friends, I realized that my period was weeks late. I wasn't paying attention to the calendar. I stopped tracking my cycle long ago.

I was vomiting a lot. Maybe it wasn't the flu after all.

I decided to take a pregnancy test. Sure enough, I was pregnant. Fear set in.

I didn't know where Craig was to tell him. I'd find him later. I decided to take a walk to calm my nerves.

Positive pregnancy test still in hand, I opened the camper door. There was Craig. Without looking, I chucked the stick at him and stormed down the sidewalk.

"Do you want me to walk with you?" he called after me while holding up the positive pregnancy test.

"No, I need to be alone," I yelled back over my shoulder as I made my way to the street, an unconscious decision to push him away.

I walked and begged and prayed some more.

Jesus, I can't lose this baby. I can't handle another loss. We've already lost everything. I can't lose anything else.

Peace instantly flooded my heart. I knew this peace was the Lord's presence. It wasn't a promise that everything would work out the way I wanted it to. It was the promise of peace, knowing that no matter what happened, I would survive it, because I have a God who cares about our sorrow. After all, Jesus is called "The Man of Sorrows."

I called Rachel, the same friend who told me that I would have a baby years earlier. This time, I let her talk about her day as I was still internally processing.

Then I blurted out, "I'm pregnant!"

"What?!" she exclaimed. "How did you let me talk for 20 minutes before interrupting me!? This is something you should tell me first! Don't let a girl go on and on while you're holding onto that kind of news!" she laughed.

I chuckled at her response. She was right. This wasn't the kind of thing to hold onto. Maybe that meant more than she even intended.

Fear isn't the kind of thing to hold onto. Fear of the unknown, fear of losing another baby, fear of uncertainty.

That night, Craig and I went to sleep with the decision that fear would not rule us, no matter how long I was pregnant.

In the morning, I called my doctor's office to let them know I was pregnant. I immediately drove to the hospital's pharmacy to pick up progesterone and get bloodwork done.

The following day, I received the long-awaited call that my HCG hormones were at above-normal levels. Maybe I was further along than I'd thought since I wasn't tracking my cycle anymore.

It was a miracle to hear that I had such strong levels! Only time would tell if they would keep getting stronger.

The God of Peace, which surpasses all understanding, was making Himself known to me.

I did not have peace that this baby would make it into my arms, but I did have peace that no matter the storm, God would be in it with me.

Each day that I woke up still pregnant, there was a sigh of relief. There were no symptoms of a miscarriage, yet.

Please, Jesus, let this baby be Victoria Faith

It was my prayer every second of every day. It was a declaration to stave off anxiety. It was a prayer of relief that no signs of losing this little one were occurring. It was my mega-faith, guttural prayer when no other words would come.

Three days later, I went in for more bloodwork to compare my previous HCG hormones. The results were astounding.

The nurse called to inform me of the news.

Without any special diets, ovulation testing, or medical interventions, it was confirmed. I was still pregnant!

The deepest sigh of relief came over my body, my mind, and my soul when I heard her words, "This baby seems to be thriving, Linni."

The nurse quickly asked me if I could make it to an ultrasound appointment, and I almost leapt through the phone. "Absolutely! When is the earliest I can come?"

MISUNDERSTANDING

Craig and I arrived at the doctor's office, located in the hospital. The same location where I delivered Mikayla Hope. The same office where I had miscarried multiple babies. The same office that could deliver the best and worst kinds of news at any given moment.

Holding onto hope that this baby would make it, I walked into the exam room. The fear threatened to undo me as if it were waiting on the sidelines, ready to jump in at any moment. I undressed and placed the blue paper blanket around my lower body.

The PA came in with my file in her hand. This PA was new to me. She sat down on a little rolling stool and placed my file on her lap.

Never looking up from her lap, she asked, "Is there any history of cancer in your family?"

I was caught off guard.

Geez. Why is she asking me this while I'm half-naked? Awkward.

"Yes, my mom had cancer twice, both melanoma, but it was caught early, back when I was in elementary school."

"How old is she now?" the PA asked.

"My mom?"

"Yes."

"She's dead."

It was the first time the PA looked up at me. We locked eyes. It was the first time I said those words so coldly. I was perplexed as to why we were discussing cancer and death when all I wanted to know was whether or not I had a living baby in my womb.

The PA broke her eye contact and stumbled through her words, trying to explain herself. I fumbled through an apology, trying to undo the awkward moment. Neither one of us really wanted to look each other in the eye again.

She continued, "How many pregnancies have you had?"

"This is my ninth pregnancy," I answered with a surreal calmness and confidence.

The PA looked at me as if she had seen a ghost. "Are all of them living with you?" she asked.

"Um...I've had seven miscarriages and one live birth, if that's what you mean," I replied.

Geez Louise! How did she enter this room and not look at the chart? Isn't it written in my chart? My chart is the size of a medical textbook at this point, and it's in her lap, for crying out loud!

She handed me two pamphlets on fetal congenital abnormalities. I stared down at the pamphlets in my hand as if I were in a horror film.

I slowly turned one over to the back to see the phrase, "medical termination of pregnancy." I looked up at her and said, "Are you for real? I'm here to see if this baby has a heartbeat, and you are handing me a pamphlet on terminating my baby?"

She returned my stare, her eyes wide. She backed her stool into the farthest corner of the room.

With my voice as steady as I could muster and anger spewing from my eyes, I spit out the words, "Please consider reading my chart next time before handing me another pamphlet like this."

She immediately stood up from her stool, nodded her head yes, looked down at the ground, and left the room as fast as she could.

Craig looked at me and teasingly said, "Calm down, killer. She's not the enemy."

I took a deep breath, and with that, I could feel my blood pulsating in my neck. My beloved doctor waltzed into the room, not knowing I had just unloaded a verbal assault on his new PA.

He wasted no time in starting the ultrasound—the all-too-familiar Beast of Truth. The machine that held my life in its hands. Would the Beast tell me there was a heartbeat? Would the Beast tell me if my hopes of another baby girl in my arms would come true? Or would the Beast yield another fatal blow?

The torturous machine lit up as it turned on. My eyes were glued to the screen. I knew exactly what to look for. I found the pregnancy sac before the doctor announced it.

I saw a squirmy little fetus inside that sac. I started to weep before the doctor even said a word.

Craig squeezed my hand with tears in his eyes. We were pregnant. Eight weeks pregnant. Unknowingly, I was already pregnant when our friend had the dream that I would be pregnant. Only God.

The doctor turned on the sound for us to hear the heartbeat.

Lub-dub, lub-dub, lub-dub

The most beautiful sound in the world.

Victoria Faith is coming.

We wouldn't need a gender reveal at 20 weeks to confirm what we already knew. We only needed an eight-week ultrasound to know that this little girl, our long-awaited answer to prayer, was growing within me.

In that room, with my feet up on those awful stirrups, I exhaled the simplest of prayers. "Thank you, Jesus."

Romans 4:17b — "...God ...gives life to the dead and calls into being things that were not."

My doctor asked me if I wanted to come back in two weeks or in four weeks.

Faith must have taken over me, because much to my own surprise, I heard myself say, "I'll come back in four weeks."

The following day, I couldn't contain my excitement during a meeting at work. I knew there was still a chance I would miscarry. I didn't want my colleagues to be in the dark after I'd had so many doctor's appointments while pregnant with Mikayla Hope, knowing that if I had to rush to the hospital, they would need to cover my classes.

I blurted out, "I'm pregnant! We have a heartbeat!"

My co-workers weren't your normal, everyday co-workers. These colleagues had been with me through all but one miscarriage and my entire pregnancy with Mikayla Hope. We had worked together for the last seven years, sharing lunches and coffee dates, the occasional weekend hike through Griffith Park, and the hard moments of working with teenagers.

These co-workers were more like family than colleagues. It didn't feel right to keep a secret longer than I needed to.

With my sudden outburst, my co-worker, Laura, matched my excitement and shouted just as loudly back at me, "I want to throw you a baby shower!"

Laura didn't hold back her excitement for me. She didn't let the past miscarriages rob her of joy. She threw caution to the wind and joined me on the journey of hiding hope. The hope that this promised baby would come when circumstances were screaming the opposite of His promises.

I hid her response in my heart. It meant the world to me that she believed right along with me that Victoria Faith was coming.

FIGHT FOR
PEACE

For the next four weeks as we waited for our next appointment, I had no signs of miscarrying. I staved off anxiety by holding onto the name "Victoria Faith."

Laughing at myself for actually saying I could wait four whole weeks to see my little nugget again, I wanted x-ray vision to see my baby girl growing within me. Each night, I fell asleep with a sigh of relief that we had survived another day.

The chance that I could lose this baby was in the back of my mind, and yet a prayer of *"Lord, give me your faith that my arms will hold this baby"* was on my tongue and in my spirit day and night.

Jesus met me in my hiding and waiting, in the early hours of the morning when I couldn't sleep on the camper table bed. He met me exactly as I was. He had no agenda with me but for me to accept His hand. I was walking by faith and I knew that my next step would be solid if I kept my eyes on Him.

At 12 weeks of gestation, we had another ultrasound. The Beast of Truth revealed our precious little miracle yet again, showing us that God is victoriously faithful to make good on His promise.

This pregnancy was night-and-day different from my pregnancy with Mikayla Hope. I had very little morning sickness. I had no bleeding or spotting. I only had two ultrasounds and no other symptoms of miscarrying.

By 13 weeks, we decided to be brave by telling people outside our little circle that we were pregnant. The friends who had walked closely with us through our miscarriages, who were extremely aware of our circumstances of living in the camper, were overjoyed with our news.

But the people who were in the nosebleed section of our lives, mostly the church ladies who we would occasionally see, were cautious in their response to us when we told them we were pregnant. They didn't want to see me in pain again if I miscarried.

Geez, if I'm not cautious in sharing my excitement, why are you trying to shield my heart by your lack of enthusiasm? Follow my lead, ladies.

I realized not everyone was invited along for our journey that had been forged by hiding and finding hope over and over again, but sometimes I didn't know who was *not* invited until they uninvited themselves with heartless comments and quips.

One man jeered at us, saying, "God never said her name would be Victoria Faith; the baby will be a boy, and you'll call him 'Victor.'"

When he said this, I stomped my foot, stared him down from across the room, and rebutted, "Watch what God does."

It was devastating to have people who we thought

were along for our journey jab us for our faith.

> *Psalm 23:5 — "You prepare a table before me in the presence of my enemies. You anoint my head with oil; my cup overflows."*

However, the more opposition we faced for saying this baby was Victoria Faith, the more my faith was firm that THIS baby was coming.

She was our promised baby girl. I became even more bold in proclaiming that Victoria Faith was in my womb.

SUNDAY MORNING MESS

As was the custom in our little church, Craig and I pulled one of our pastors aside before a Sunday service to ask if we could share about Victoria Faith coming during the worship time with the congregation. Typically, this was a time of highlighting what God was saying to the people. It seemed fitting for us to share our testimony of a miracle. As a matter of order, it was also understood that before a person shares, they need to ask permission first.

Our pastor knew about our journey of infertility, miscarriages and a miracle baby. To our utter shock, he told us with straight coldness, "No, you cannot share. Just wait until the ultrasound, when you know for sure it is a girl, and then you can share."

I stared him down, blinking a million times in disbelief.

Did I just hear him correctly?

The same man who had prayed for colds to be healed years ago—the prayer that healed Mikayla when she was in my womb—was the same man who would not let us testify that we knew Victoria Faith was coming? He needed to see an ultrasound first?

I shook my head in a mixture of horror and disbelief. The one place where I expected miracles to be expected became the one place where my miracle was shunned. The lack of faith from our pastor was more than my heart could handle.

What a mess.

If my faith was larger than my pastor's faith, then he was clearly not invited along for this journey, either. Our journey with the Lord was truly ours and no one else's, apparently.

The pastor never gave an explanation beyond the one he gave that day, and I never asked for one. It was another sign to me that our theology was changing. The God of the Bible was not a distant God, but a God who walked with us in our everyday lives.

Even though we didn't have a religious label for our experiences, we were becoming more outspoken in our expression with each miracle we experienced.

We just knew that God was not a distant God who passively controlled all aspects of our lives, but that He was a God who actively participated with us in our grief, joy, and peace.

He was a God who spoke to our hearts. He was the God of the Bible. The Bible was a living Word, not an ancient textbook for expository sermons.

> *Hebrews 2:13a — ... "I will put my trust in Him."*

I became disillusioned by our pastor's pride when

he challenged my faith as if he needed to protect God's reputation.

Are all pastors like this?

I began to believe that I could only respect a pastor for his job title, but not for his guidance in my life. I made a vow to myself that I would never let another pastor give me advice, neither as a spiritual guide nor as a mentor. Yet, God was waiting to redeem this, too.

FINALLY HOME

The next few weeks of pregnancy were as uneventful as watching a pot of water boil, thankfully.

I was no longer counting the days I was pregnant, but the weeks. My belly started to show. The embarrassment that I was visibly pregnant while living in a pop-up camper was starting to become a real source of uneasiness for me.

I was counting down the days on the calendar for our nonexistent move-out date. We were in month 14 of living in the camper, and we still had not gathered the required funds for a deposit on a new place.

Like clockwork, every time we saved enough money, we felt like Jesus would ask us to give it away. By this point, we had given more money away with one income than we had when we had two incomes.

We were learning generosity in the craziest of ways, giving away our last dollar over and over again with each paycheck. God was teaching us that He alone is our provider.

At the same time, there were no prospects in sight for an apartment. The uncertainty I felt about not knowing where we would live when this baby came kicked in. I was no longer afraid to miscarry—I was afraid we would be living in a camper forever.

Lord, You've gotta get us out of here. I feel like we are wearing out our welcome. Is Victoria going to learn how to crawl in a camper? I want a real place to live, with a kitchen and a working bathroom!

The plea for Jesus to rescue us from homelessness was audible. The desperation for us to be in our own place was running high. I clung to Jesus, hoping for a home to call our own.

On the other hand, peace replaced anxiety about this pregnancy as I looked at my growing belly and started to feel the flutter of little baby kicks against my abdomen. They felt more like butterfly movements than kicks, but they were movements nonetheless. My heart was full of gratitude that this baby had made it this far.

At my 20-week appointment with my perinatologist, the ultrasound tech asked if Craig and I wanted to know the gender of our baby.

I excitedly told her that we knew we were having a girl. "Just a mama's intuition, I guess," I told her.

"Welp," she said, "you're right! You're having a girl! Does this baby have a name, yet?"

"Victoria Faith!" Craig and I said in unison.

My faith for our baby to make it into my arms was strong. But my anxiety over our living situation was building.

By the time I was six months pregnant with Victoria Faith, we were still homeless.

It had been 17 long months of living in the camper.

It was obvious at this point that I was indeed pregnant. It was even more painfully obvious that there were no prospects for an apartment on the horizon.

God, what are you doing? Why did you bring us here?

He spoke to my heart, *"Wherever I tell you to go, you will go. Whatever I tell you to do, you will do. I have been teaching you to follow me, no matter the cost."*

Why did you bring us to the camper, God?

He whispered, *"To pray. Wherever your feet go, you have authority. Each family you lived with needed your prayers of intercession for them."*

I finally understood why we were asked to give up our house. I was at peace with our season of homelessness.

Out of the blue, just like God likes to do, we were surprised with a phone call from an apartment management company in Los Angeles, wanting to interview Craig for a job. He had submitted a resume months earlier but had heard nothing.

This job meant that we could live in an apartment with compensated rent in exchange for Craig working onsite at one of their apartment buildings. But there was a catch. The only opening they had was a one-bedroom apartment.

There was a rumor that this management company didn't like for their managers to have children for some reason. If you had children, they were harsher with you on other aspects of your job. Time would tell if that was true.

Craig always did well in interviews. I knew he would get the job, but the company didn't know I was pregnant. We didn't even know if they would allow a family of four to live in a one-bedroom apartment.

Craig came home from the interview saying that they were holding off on making a decision until they met me.

I was devastated. My belly holding a miracle could be the same belly that would keep us homeless. The thought of it not working out seemed unbearable.

The night before my interview, I tried on different coats to see which one would hide my round belly the best.

Craig reasoned, "Babe, if they aren't going to hire us because they don't want four of us in a one-bedroom, then God will give us another option."

I wanted to believe him so badly, but at the same time, we knew multiple people who worked for this company. We knew the rumors. The chance of them hiring us while I was pregnant was slim to none.

The following morning, I drove to the company's office. I looked at the clock in my car. It read "7:59." I wrapped my belly as best I could in my coat, walked to the office, and knocked on the door. No one answered.

I knocked again. A very flustered woman opened the door. She scanned my body from head to toe. Her eyes moved across my belly and back up to my eyes.

"Hello, I'm Linni, Craig's wife. I'm here for the interview," I said.

"Oh, you're here. Do you have any tattoos?" she asked.

Taken aback, I replied, "Umm, no..."

"Do you smoke or drink?"

"No," I said, shaking my head from side to side.

"Okay, good. We'll let you know our decision in one week. Bye."

She slammed the door in my face. Completely shocked by the questions and the candor with which she spoke, I walked back to my car trying to figure out what had just happened.

As I slid into my car's seat, starting the ignition, I looked at the clock. It read "8:02."

Those three minutes determined my fate?! Clearly she saw that I was pregnant. This was going to be a long week waiting for a decision.

One week went by. We had not heard from the company. Two weeks went by. Still no word. I wanted Craig to call the company, but he felt we needed to just pray that they would hire us.

Three weeks went by. Still nothing. Radio silence. The act of waiting for this job while I continued to grow more round with each week was an extreme exercise in patience.

Finally, after three weeks of waiting and praying that this would be our answer out of homelessness, we got the phone call. "Sorry it took us so long to get back with you; we had a few things we needed to figure out. Can you move in two weeks?" she asked.

"Yes, absolutely we can!"

After 18 months of living in the camper, we moved our furniture out of storage and into our one-bedroom apartment when I was 30 weeks pregnant with Victoria Faith. It had been 22 long months since we had slept in our own bed.

Jesus was showing us yet again how faithful He was, even in the midst of our uncertainty. He promised us this little girl and that we would not be homeless forever.

We were finally home.

Genesis 28:15 — "I am with you and will watch over you wherever you go, and I will bring you back to this land. I will not leave you until I have done what I have promised you."

TEXTBOOK
PERFECT

One week after we moved into our new apartment, my co-worker and dear friend, Laura, stayed true to her word and threw me the sweetest little baby shower a girl could ever ask for!

Gray paper cut-outs of little baby elephants were placed throughout Laura's adorable house. They were strung on garland, propped up on tables, and dangling from her ceiling.

Women near and far drove to celebrate this miracle baby. My friends and co-workers, who had encircled me during all the heartache of infertility, arrived with gifts in their hands. Even the church ladies, who had stayed on the outskirts hoping we would not miscarry, showed up, too.

We all crowded into Laura's living room. We came from all walks of life. All religions, including non-religious backgrounds. Each of us holding hope for Craig and me to have this baby. All in one room together, celebrating the promised baby, Victoria Faith.

There, among the cake and cookies, was the

sweetest of memories: the practical gifts of love—box after box of baby diapers stacked on top of each other from the floor to the ceiling. There would be enough diapers to carry Victoria Faith through to adulthood.

At 39 weeks pregnant, I arrived in the labor and delivery wing quite round and ready to pop. A c-section was scheduled to take place a few hours later.

The nurse hooked me up to the contraction monitor. She looked at the chart and then back at my calm demeanor.

"Um, Mrs. Weishaar, you're having strong contractions. Can you feel that? We might need to get you to an OR quickly."

"Nope, I don't feel a thing," I laughed.

"Hmmm, your pain tolerance must be very high."

I had not felt any contractions at that point. Little did I know that this question of pain tolerance would foreshadow upcoming events in my life.

The nurse held my IV drip bag as I was escorted to the OR. I finally started to feel the contractions. With each contraction, I stopped walking. By the time I was sitting on the OR table, the anesthesiologist came into the room and started talking.

Blah, blah, blah…

"Sorry, doctor, I didn't hear a word you said," I said calmly.

There was an awkward pause. The nurse told him I was having contractions.

"Oh! Well, then let's get started!"

He rushed to get me prepped. I warned him about my reaction to my last epidural.

"Oh, good to know! I'll fix that for you."

At our previous appointment, Craig had asked our doctor if he could watch the c-section. To my utter shock, the doctor said, "Sure! As long as you promise not to faint!"

As the blue curtain was being raised above my head, Craig peered over to watch the doctor perform the surgery.

My doctor was a teaching doctor, so he naturally started telling Craig every step he was taking, to which I yelled, "I can hear you! I don't want to know a thing! Not. A. Thing!"

The doctor lowered his voice and continued explaining what he was doing as if Craig were a surgeon in training.

My blood boiled with anger as Craig was not attentive to me, his wife, on that table, but to the process of how a child was born via c-section.

For me, it was yet another example of Craig being there for me physically, but not mentally or emotionally. *Unseen.*

As I searched for comfort in Craig's eyes, I saw the reflection of my innards in his eyeglasses. I yelled, "Hey! Are you here for me or for the Discovery Channel?"

"Sorry, Linni, this is just so cool!" he responded, unphased by my sarcasm.

Unlike Mikayla Hope's entrance into the world, I instantly heard Victoria Faith cry a loud, healthy cry. They held her over the blue curtain for me to see. I watched her body turn from purple to pink right before my eyes. Our long-awaited declaration that God is victoriously faithful was finally in my sight.

The assisting female doctor said, "Oh my, that is an ugly uterus!"

My doctor said, "Yeah, she had surgery to remove a septum and seven miscarriages. This baby is a miracle!"

"I would say so," she replied as she started sewing me up. I heard her mutter, "How in the world did she carry this baby to full-term?"

I was 30 years old. Mikayla was a couple weeks shy of five years old. After almost three years of waiting for our promise to come, our second miracle baby was announced in the OR.

When I held Victoria for the first time, a sigh of relief exhaled from my lungs. I connected with her immediately. I was at ease knowing that this little girl was here to stay. My body didn't react to the epidural, either. Minus the announcement of an ugly uterus, it was a textbook-perfect pregnancy and delivery.

Redemption.

MIC DROP

After Victoria was born, we said goodbye to our little church. We both felt like we had outgrown the church we had attended for the last eight years, as if our shoes were too tiny to walk out of the service comfortably each Sunday morning.

On our last Sunday, a woman walked up to the prophecy mic, bypassing the pastors' row, and said, "Craig and Linni taught an entire church how to hear the voice of God. Victoria Faith is a testimony that He still speaks today."

Mic drop.

Craig and I glanced at each other. Our eyes met. Right there we knew why we had been there all these years.

Isaiah 55:11 — "...[S]o is my word that goes out from my mouth: It will not return to me empty..."

The first Sunday after leaving, we stayed home.

Being so involved in the children's ministry, it was a breath of fresh air to just be home, still in our pajamas on a Sunday at noon.

The following Sunday, Craig suggested we start looking for a new church.

"I'm churched out," I said. "You can go ahead and look for another church without me. I'm sitting this one out."

He looked at me as one who understood, but asked, "For how long?"

"Forever."

He and five-year-old Mikayla set out to attend a church down the road from us. It was a large church. He came home and said that I would love the worship music and asked if I would come with him the next Sunday.

I told him, "Nope. Religion is for you, not for me."

I didn't want anyone to know me. I just wanted my faith to stay intact without the verbal backlash of not always having the right words to say to a church lady or to a pastor.

Week after week, Craig came home so full of joy. He loved the services. He loved the atmosphere. He loved the people.

Seeing his joy finally broke me. I heard the Lord whisper to my heart, *"I didn't make you to stand on the sidelines."*

I gave in and said, "Okay, fine. I'll go."

I was half-excited and half-frightened out of my mind.

I resolved that in this new church, no one would need to know our story of nine pregnancies, seven miscarriages, and two miracle babies. It was too much to be known as an infertile woman with a broken body, who just happened to have two kids. My plan was to sit in the back pew of the church and just blend in.

Go in. Sit down. Leave early. No conversing. With. Anyone.

GOLD-PAINTED LEAF

Saturday night, the night before I went to this new church with Craig, I had a vivid dream.

In the dream, I opened a door to a church's foyer. I had never seen this church before. As soon as I stepped inside the church, an elderly woman with pure white, short curly hair ran towards me with open arms!

"You're here! You're here! You're my daughter! Come with me. I have to show you something!" she exclaimed.

I ran behind her as she rushed into a small room. The room glistened as if an ethereal angel was standing in the doorway. On the far wall to my left was a hand-painted mural of a tree. Each branch had hundreds of leaves on it, each leaf with a person's name written in gold lettering.

On the floor were real brown leaves, piled high around the painted mural on the wall. The woman scanned the pile of leaves. She spotted the one she was looking for. She bent down to pick up a brown leaf off of the floor and said to me, "See, this leaf has your name on it. You are a part of our family."

She then placed the brown leaf on a branch of the mural. The leaf instantly turned green as it touched and melted into the painting. It looked as if the leaf had always been there.

My name appeared in calligraphy on the gold-painted leaf.

Her eyes pierced my soul when she looked at me, acknowledging all of the pain I felt from being chided by the church ladies, women who were her same age. Then, she motioned for me to sit on a cushion that appeared out of nowhere. She put her arm around my shoulder and turned me to the opposite wall, which had a TV mounted on it.

"Look at the TV," she instructed.

When I turned my head to look at the TV, it displayed a timer from an old black and white movie countdown. 3...2...1... Each number appeared on the screen and then disappeared.

"It is time to say goodbye to your former pastors; they are retiring now," she gently said.

In the dream, I exhaled all of the disappointment I had felt about our experiences with church over the years. I knew it was time to start the forgiveness process.

"Welcome to the family. You are home," she said as she hugged me tightly.

I awoke the next morning with an excitement that maybe, just maybe, this could be the church for me. I walked into the new church half-expecting to have a woman with white hair run to greet me, but that didn't happen.

Instead, I opened the doors to the sanctuary and

was almost blown over by the air conditioning. Or was it the Holy Spirit? Or...? Who knows what pushed my body back as I opened that door. It was a force that shook me to my core.

We sat in the back row of the auditorium. During the worship service, I scanned the large room. People were raising their hands in worship. Some women were crying with smiles on their faces, unconcerned about who saw their emotions.

I desperately wanted to cry like that. Jealousy took hold of me. I was very aware that I had made a vow years ago that no one would ever see me cry again.

Lord, teach me how to cry like that.

It had been a long time since I had freely let tears stream down my face, but the tears didn't come that day.

I thought I was hiding in this massive church by sitting in the back, but a pastor made a beeline for us almost immediately as we stepped back into the foyer after the service. I had nine-month-old Victoria on my hip.

She commented, "I am so drawn to your baby! She is full of the Holy Spirit. She is a Seer."

Seriously, God! You can't let me hide at all!? This is totally unfair! I don't want anyone to know my story and this lady is already picking up on it! And what in the world is a Seer?

I took a deep breath, knowing deep down I needed to share our testimony of Victoria Faith. I then shared about not being allowed to testify that Victoria Faith was coming before an ultrasound confirmed she was a girl. This new pastor's eyes widened with disbelief.

She grabbed my hand. "On behalf of the Body of Christ and pastors who have not covered you well, I want to stand in the gap and ask for your forgiveness for failing you. Please continue to share your story. The Body of Christ needs it."

Psalm 68:6a — "God sets the lonely in families..."

"Thank you," I said in return.
I felt seen and heard. My heart shifted.
I'm home.

GRAVE
CLOTHES

Victoria was close to turning a year old. Watching my baby learn to walk triggered a desire for more children without warning.

Each time I set the dinner table, it felt like there were family members missing around it. I didn't know why.

Anytime I saw a pregnant woman, I wanted to cry, but the tears wouldn't form. Every time I was invited to a baby shower, I RSVP'd "With Regrets," even if I had no other plans. Little did I know that this was trauma surfacing.

Despite knowing that miscarrying was a real possibility, I was holding onto hope for the future of more children in one hand, while holding onto joy in the present with my miracle babies in the other. The two conflicting ideas caused turmoil within me.

I couldn't explain, even to myself, the desire for more children to be seated around our dining room table, especially when I had two healthy children. So many women were praying for just one healthy baby. It didn't seem right to want more kids.

One evening, Craig walked into our apartment shouting at the top of his lungs, "Linni! What are you doing?! You're going to kill our children!"

"What!?" Anger instantly boiled over at his unwarranted accusation. Daggers slashed open my heart.

"I can't trust you with our children! You're going to *kill* them!" he shouted even louder.

Shocked that my husband would yell at me, and even more shocked that he accused me of being neglectful, all the lies I had believed years earlier flooded back to the surface of my being. Lies I thought I had dismantled reared their ugly heads.

I looked towards the desk in our living room and saw that Victoria had crawled under it. She was happily playing with an electric cord. Craig rushed to grab Victoria away from the live outlet.

I knew it. Craig thinks I am a horrible mother. I killed all of our children. My miscarried babies knew I would be a terrible mother, and that's why they didn't stay in my womb.

I jabbed, "Well, you're never around! You're a neglectful husband! Do you even see me?"

We wielded our weaponized tongues at each other's armored hearts well into the night. All the years of disconnection had come to a head.

We need help.

That same week, we began individual therapy sessions to figure out why, all of a sudden, old wounds were resurfacing. *Hidden trauma.*

I arrived at a therapist's office. The tiny room was painted a minty green color. It looked more like a sterile dentist's office than a warm therapist's office. The dread of what would come out of my mouth in the most vulnerable of moments kept me on high alert.

Would this woman shame me like so many other women? Would she allow me to talk without giving ridiculous advice?

I willed my body to sit on the gray, oversized couch that took up three-quarters of her office. Being a petite person, the couch cushions enveloped me. The depth of the couch was so great that I couldn't bend my knees. My legs didn't touch the ground. They stuck out like a kindergartener's legs wiggling in the seat at the principal's office.

I had two options: sit at the edge of the couch with my feet touching the floor, or sit back into the couch with my back supported. I chose the latter.

I felt like I was about to get a tooth pulled, half-lying, half-sitting on that ridiculously huge couch. I changed my mind and scooted to the edge of the couch.

The therapist came into the room with a confident, eccentric air about her. Her dark, Middle Eastern tresses were flying about her face. After the usual pleasantries, she jumped right in as if I'd been seeing her for years.

"Do you always dress like this?"

"Dress like what?" I asked incredulously, trying not to be totally offended by her blunt question.

"Dress like you're going to a funeral," she stated without blinking an eye.

I looked down at my feet. My eyes glanced from my toes to my shoulders, taking inventory.

Black heels. Black pants. Black shirt.

I looked over at my black purse sitting next to me. "I don't dress like this all the time. I'm an interpreter. It's our uniform to wear black," I quipped.

Not believing me, she said slowly, "Typically, when women dress the way you are dressed—all black, no jewelry, no painted nails—they are in mourning. Wearing all black is a sign that you're wearing grave clothes."

"I wear black a lot, but I have color in my wardrobe, too. *These* are not grave clothes," I fought back. *Denial.*

"Really? Are you sure about that?"

"Yes," I shot back, getting more defensive the longer she stared at me.

"Okay, then, next week, bring me clothes that are not black," she challenged me confidently.

I drove home determined to bring back my entire wardrobe full of color. I arrived home and swung open my closet doors. I desperately combed through my wardrobe, trying to find any ounce of color I could.

Nothing. How could that be?

I jerked open my dresser drawers, each drawer showing that black was indeed the only color in my wardrobe.

Desperate to prove this eccentric therapist wrong, I found one blue t-shirt from my school's baseball team.

Aha! I found one color that's not black; I'll show her!

Even so, I secretly wondered if she was onto something. I had not had a miscarriage in more than three and a half years, though.

Maybe I am still in mourning.

The following week, I walked back into her office with my tail between my legs, showing her my one blue t-shirt. "See, I do have color in my wardrobe!" I laughed.

Lamentations 3:32 — "Though he brings grief, he will show compassion, so great is his unfailing love."

She grinned and said, "I told you so. Now that you're ready to talk...tell me about your grave clothes." This was the beginning of my counseling journey.

BRIGHT LIGHT

When Victoria turned two years old, Craig's career was going well. I left my job at the high school and started my own freelance business. We both felt like therapy had been a good investment in ourselves and our marriage. Life was peaceful and calm.

The Lord started highlighting women I'd pass in the street or at church who I knew in my spirit had miscarried or were experiencing infertility. They would "light up" as if someone had turned on a bright light behind them.

Over time, while attending our massive church, women would ask me to pray for them to have a baby. I laid hands on them, and seven of them conceived.

> *Mark 16:17a, 18b — "And these signs will accompany those who believe: In my name they will drive out demons; ... they will place their hands on sick people, and they will get well."*

One day, Victoria was playing on the floor in a Chick-Fil-A play area while Mikayla, who had just turned seven, was sliding down the yellow slide.

A tall woman with long, black hair wearing a white cable-knit sweater came in with a little boy who was about five or six. She sat down next to me on the tiny, red bench.

I looked over to say, "Hello." I instantly caught her half-smile and saw a pain in her eyes as she looked at Victoria Faith. I knew exactly what that smile meant.

I pointed to Victoria, who was now climbing the stairs. "This little one is my miracle baby. Over there on the slide is my other miracle baby. I was told twice that I couldn't have children."

Nodding her head, she said, "He's my nephew. I don't have any children. I wish I could have a baby."

We chatted for a while, exchanging heartfelt stories of our similar pain. I knew the Lord brought her to me to give her hope that day.

Since our shoulders were already touching on the tiny, little red bench, I asked her if I could give her a hug. She nodded her head, "Yes."

We embraced. Her heart's desire was seen. I was overjoyed to be a listener of her story and to hear her heart.

"You must be a believer," I said.

She said, "Yes."

I prayed a prayer of declaration that she would have a child.

These kinds of encounters became commonplace. I knew my greatest misery was becoming my greatest ministry. I could freely give the gift of comfort and the gift of presence amid unexplainable heartache while also giving the gift of hope. Comforting women gave my journey purpose.

2 Corinthians 1:4 — "[He] who comforts us in all our troubles, so that we can comfort those in any trouble with the comfort we ourselves receive from God."

LUCKY NUMBER
TEN

After Victoria's third birthday, we moved into a two-bedroom apartment. Now that we had a larger home, it felt like a good time to explore other ways of expanding our family.

During my teenage years, I had the privilege of teaching English and ASL to toddlers who were adopted from China. That experience was a highlight of my youth, a source of wonder and delight that stayed with me for years to come.

Later on, as I pursued a career in education, my heart was drawn to those who had suffered in the foster care system. Being there for my students, offering a glimmer of hope and support, was a true privilege that filled me with joy and purpose.

Craig and I had always dreamed of becoming resource parents for kids in the foster care system, as well as adopting, but early in our marriage we didn't meet the minimum age requirements when we first explored those avenues. Now that we were older the timing seemed right.

I was in awe of our friends who had navigated the

arduous adoption journey. And my heart went out to our friends who were supporting reunification of families in foster care.

Craig and I completed the 30 hours of required training for foster parents and started our home study only to find out that our bedrooms were one square inch too small to qualify as a foster home. Even domestic and foreign adoption would need to be put on hold until we moved into a three-bedroom home.

With rent in Los Angeles being astronomical for a three-bedroom apartment, exploring ways to enlarge our family came to a dead end rather quickly. Moving didn't seem to be a viable option.

The shock that a bedroom size was another closed door made it feel like I miscarried again. The dream of expanding our family in other ways crashed and burned.

We decided that we would try for baby number three, or ten, depending on how one viewed it.

We knew the odds of us getting pregnant quickly were slim to none. But to our utter surprise, a month after our decision to try for another baby, a pregnancy test showed two strong pink lines!

Our tenth pregnancy! Lucky number ten!

I wasn't worried at all about miscarrying this baby. The fear had been conquered.

However, shortly after finding out I was pregnant, I woke up spotting and cramping. Devastation hit. Just when I no longer feared the worst, the worst came true...again.

Will this be my journey? Will this be the story that defines me? I feel as though I am an infertile mother of two. Why can't I just be happy with two children?

After a few hours, I couldn't stand it any longer. I didn't want to sit in disillusionment with my body failing me over and over.

We had plans to go to a Fourth of July barbeque with friends from our new church. I didn't want to cancel on them.

I had the attitude of "been there, done that" with so many miscarriages that I rationalized, *The eighth miscarriage wasn't so bad. I will be fine. I just want a few hours away from our lives to take my mind off of this impending doom of death.*

We drove to Melina and Jason's house for the barbeque. I ate and laughed, and for a brief moment, I forgot about my pain.

Melina needed to go to the grocery store to buy more ice cream, so I tagged along. While we were in the cold dessert aisle looking for vanilla ice cream, I confided in her that I was miscarrying.

She instantly hugged me, saying, "I'm so sorry."

That's all I needed to hear. That's all I ever wanted to hear.

We grabbed the ice cream and drove back to her house. After eating my second hotdog of the day, my stomach ballooned. I was so uncomfortable that we drove home early, missing the fireworks.

SUPERHERO CAPE

I jumped into a hot bath as soon as we got home. I stayed in the bathtub until the water turned cold. When I stood up to grab a towel, the abdominal pain was so great that I started vomiting.

This is horrible gas!

I was more annoyed with the miscarriage than I was concerned for my bloated stomach. I was annoyed that my body was broken. Annoyed that a 33-year-old woman couldn't carry another child, my tenth child.

I discovered that lying down in a hot tub of water was my only relief. The pain would go away, and my nausea would stop. But as soon as the water became cold, I'd stand up, and the vomiting would resume.

By 3:00 a.m., Craig came into the bathroom. "You need to go to the emergency room."

Fierce with anger, I sneered through my teeth, "There is no way I need to go to the ER. One, I am miscarrying, and there is nothing they can do for me, and two, terrible gas hit me at the barbeque. Once it passes, I will be fine."

At 3:30 a.m. he said, "Linni, you've been saying 'Oh

dear Jesus' for the last eight hours. You're *going* to the ER."

"Fine," I said with the attitude of a two-year-old in the middle of a tantrum. I might as well have crossed my arms over my chest, but my whole body hurt so badly I couldn't move quickly.

"I'll drive myself, since there's no one to watch the girls," I told him.

I slowly got dressed and drove to the hospital.

They're just going to make fun of me for having gas. It is ridiculous that Craig is making me go to the hospital.

Much to my surprise, the ER was completely empty on the night of July 4th! I was shocked. I walked hunched over to the admitting desk, where about five or six nurses sat, all lounging around as if business was slow like this every night.

One man behind the desk asked, "What brings you in here tonight?"

I clearly couldn't stand up all the way. The pain wrapped around my entire body.

"I am miscarrying and have pain around my back and abdomen," I replied, trying my best to smile.

He waved his arm back towards all of his spiritless colleagues and said, "Okay, well, we can bring you back right away. Which one of us do you want to help you?"

"Which one of you is the most bored?" I joked. It garnered a chuckle from all of them. A young lad shot his hand into the air. He escorted me back to an empty room.

After I was settled into a hospital bed, an ultrasound was done on my uterus and abdomen. I was offered morphine.

"I'll just take Advil," I said, knowing my body didn't handle medications very well. I didn't want to repeat any of those experiences.

The nurse said, "Honey, Advil isn't going to cut this pain. You need something stronger."

I was given something through an IV that almost instantaneously made me think I was 100% back to normal and could go home.

The ER doctor came into the room to ask me questions. I joked around with him about having one too many hotdogs at a barbeque. He laughed and said to me, "You didn't really come in here for a miscarriage, did you?"

"No," I admitted sheepishly.

"Yeah, I didn't think so," he nodded.

"The gas pain was so bad, but I thought you would all make fun of me for having gas!" I chuckled.

I couldn't stop giggling. Clearly, whatever they gave me in that IV was working.

He asked, "Who is waiting for you in the lobby?"

"What do you mean?"

"Who drove you to the ER?"

His question finally clicked. "Oh, no one. I drove myself."

It was his turn to laugh uncontrollably.

It must be a very slow night in the ER.

"Where is your Superwoman cape?" he joked.

"Right over there. Underneath my clothes," I slyly smiled, pointing to the chair in the corner of the room.

He composed himself. He looked me straight in the

eyes. All laughter instantly vanished. "You are one tough lady; you're as tough as nails," he said.

I took the compliment like any superhero would.

He left the room to get the results of the ultrasounds. Shortly thereafter, he came back with a somber look on his face.

"Ma'am, this is not gas. Your gallbladder is extremely inflamed. You have so many gallstones that if you had ignored your pain for two more days, you would have died. You have learned to numb your pain."

The soberness of his voice caught my attention. I had unknowingly turned off my pain, both emotionally and physically, and he called me out on it.

All those years of choosing not to cry in front of others backfired. All those years of stuffing tears into my heart when women were in front of me numbed my brain. Literally.

My superhero cape almost killed me.

He recommended immediate surgery to remove my gallbladder. I asked him if there were any more conservative options. His laughter made me giggle at my own question.

"I knew you were going to ask that! No, if you want to live, you are way past the time for conservative options. Your gallbladder is infected and inflamed, and if it bursts, you could die," he explained.

I called Craig at 6:00 a.m. to tell him I was having surgery. The admissions person for the hospital came to my room and said that he had run my insurance card. They would only cover the first $50.00 of the ER bill.

"What?" I exclaimed. "Are you sure it's not that our copay is $50.00, and they cover the rest of the bill?"

"No, with the new universal health care plans in effect, this is becoming more prevalent because people are missing the deadline to sign up for health insurance when they don't work for an employer.

The insurance you have is like gap insurance. These companies look as though they are saving the day by helping those who didn't sign up for insurance before the deadline, but they are basically frauds. It happened to a friend of mine, too," he explained sympathetically.

He was right. I was self-employed. I had totally missed the universal healthcare deadline for open enrollment. I scrambled to find insurance after realizing it.

"Ok, well, can you let me go home? I can find another insurance company, and then I'll come back for the surgery," I was half-begging, half-questioning.

"No, ma'am, it's too dangerous to release you. I am so sorry. I'll see what I can do for you," he said.

For the first time since finding out I was miscarrying, I let it all out. I laid there in the hospital bed and just let the tears run down my face. There was nothing else I could do. Panic set in.

How in the world are we going to afford this!?

As the morning sun rose. I waited to be admitted, without insurance. I contacted a few people to inform them of my situation.

1) I was miscarrying.
2) I needed surgery.

3) The doctor told me if I had waited any longer, I could have died.

4) My insurance card was no good. I needed help figuring out what we could do.

I was reminded, yet again, that I was not meant to carry my burdens by myself, but that friends were there to help me. *Redemption.* I had a very strong support system.

As I waited for the surgeon to arrive, a friend came to visit me in the hospital. Craig came by with Mikayla and Victoria, too. I had an affable nurse who told me that I drove to the right hospital because it was known for helping many people in need, and if I needed medical care, I shouldn't be denied financial help. Her confidence was reassuring.

Craig was busy with the girls. We didn't connect at all. We went into our old patterns of self-sufficiency. I didn't need him. I didn't need his strength or presence to get through this. I had come to expect that he would not be there for me emotionally. I didn't realize until years later how much I had blocked him from painful parts of my emotions.

My friend Leticia called as many insurance companies as she could to see if we could get enrolled before surgery. All possibilities were dead ends.

That evening, I had surgery. When I woke up, I felt almost 100% better.

The following day, I was discharged, minus a few ounces and a gallbladder.

Once home, I couldn't get myself out of bed. The doctor's words still resonated within me. It was as if all of the years of disappointment crashed down on me. My body was paralyzed.

When the doctor asked me where my superhero cape was, it struck a chord. I knew that with this miscarriage I needed to allow myself to cry in front of others—especially in front of my husband.

My friend Rachel would tell me over the years that I needed to hang up my superhero cape and let it mend itself. Many times, this was said in regards to not allowing myself to heal after a miscarriage. Going straight back to work in the early years of miscarriages and infertility. Working long hours with babies who didn't sleep through the night. Even when I accidentally superglued my belly button shut years earlier.

She always said it with care. It was her reminder to me that I am not invincible and that being strong isn't always the best remedy for healing.

I let myself lay in bed and do nothing. I needed it. I needed it for the assurance that miracles are called miracles for a reason. I needed it for the alone time with myself. I needed it for quiet time with the Lord. I needed it to sleep. I needed it to face disappointment with new tools.

Jesus was inviting me to go deeper with Him into the Secret Place. The secret place of intimacy with the Father who had no agenda for me. In the secret place where my raw emotions of inexplicable grief were met with the Savior's healing hands.

My hope was not gone; it was just hidden under layers and layers of disappointment, beckoning me to dig deeper into the pain and allow Jesus to come in and uncover it.

I was clinging to Jesus, learning to walk by faith and not by sight in a whole new way.

By the end of three weeks, I knew I needed an even deeper level of healing. I needed to know why I felt so empty when sitting around our dinner table and why I continued to want more children, even though my body refused to cooperate. I felt bound by sorrow and depression.

Sozo

I started seeing a new therapist. She incorporated various practices into her sessions which helped me so much more than just being told I had grave clothes.

One method she used is called "SOZO," from the Greek word for "saved" or "delivered." This was a way for the Lord to uncover and address hidden root issues that needed to be healed in my life. My therapist led me in prayer. Together, we asked the Holy Spirit to show us where the pain was. Then she asked, "Where is Jesus in that pain?"

As I prayed, I immediately saw a vision of a black, English-style baby carriage from the 1800s that Jesus was pushing. Inside the baby carriage were eight little black rocks. The therapist asked me what those black rocks meant. As if I had known this my entire life, I told her, "Each rock represents each one of my miscarriages."

She asked, "Is that how God sees your miscarriages—as worthless rocks?"

With that one simple question, I started to sob uncontrollably without fear of being judged. I felt

God's love for me in a different way. I felt His grief mixed in with my grief. I felt His hope over my hope, which had been hidden in the dark recesses of my heart. His emotions gave me permission to have my own.

Instantly, the vision changed. I saw the baby carriage turn into a white, modern-day baby carriage, with eight diamonds sitting on a white pillow inside the carriage. Each diamond replaced each of the eight black rocks that had been sitting there before.

John 10:10 — "The thief comes only to steal and kill and destroy; I have come that they may have life, and have it to the full."

I realized that God didn't cause my babies' deaths. It is the enemy who steals, kills, and destroys. God was grieving for my babies right along with me.

In his book, *The Pursuit of God,* theologian A.W. Tozer said, "What comes into our minds when we think about God is the most important thing about us." I realized how deeply God cared. He mourned with me. He mourned for my losses.

He loved those eight little diamonds. Each baby was priceless and invaluable to Him. Each baby was made in His image. *I* was made in His image. My worth was not in my uterus, nor in my pain, but in my being a child of God. Tears continued to stream down my face. *Healing.*

*Luke 12:7 — "Indeed, the very hairs
of your head are all numbered. Don't
be afraid; you are worth more than
many sparrows."*

In the next appointment, the therapist and I did a second SOZO session. In this prayer time, I was finally ready to know the gender of each of our babies. Nine years earlier, I thought my mom was nuts for asking God about that. Now, curiosity struck me—I really wanted to know the genders of my babies!

As I bowed my head and asked my Heavenly Father to show me my children, I saw myself sitting in my rocking chair—the one that always reminded me of His promise, so many years earlier.

In the vision, I was holding Mikayla and Victoria at their current ages. I saw eight little blonde-haired, blue-eyed toddlers running in circles around my chair. They were playing and happy to be near me.

My babies wanted to be with me. They had joy running around my chair.

*Psalm 23:5b — "You anoint my head
with oil; my cup overflows."*

The lie I had believed of being a horrible mother and that's why my babies were gone was truly dismantled.

I started counting my children—six girls and two

boys. I saw their faces. I knew they were okay. They were in Heaven with Jesus. I'd see them again one day.

Over the course of the next six months, Craig worked on financial statements and appeals regarding my hospital bills, trying to work out payment plans. He believed God was going to make a way for us to not be burdened with this debt.

While he focused on that, I focused on healing with my new therapist. I was becoming even more honest with my feelings than I had ever allowed myself to be.

I was learning the stories of women in the Bible who were not known for their fertility, but for their willingness to say yes. For their courageous faith, radical obedience, and fierce loyalty to God.

Deborah rallied her nation against an enemy. Rahab hid the Israelite spies saving her family, while Esther thwarted the genocide of her people. Abigail shrewdly counseled King David. The Prophetess Anna prophesized the arrival of the Messiah, and Jesus honored Mary Magdalene by appearing to her first after His resurrection. I read countless accounts attesting to the valor of women of God.

One woman had no record of knowing God, yet her willingness to say yes, no matter the cost, allowed God to use her mightily. She saved a baby boy from a rushing river's stir. She raised him in the palace as her own. He later would know how to talk to a king to save his people after 400 years of slavery. Moses' adoptive mother didn't have a name recorded except, "Pharoah's daughter." A daughter of the king who changed history by simply picking up a baby boy out of a river.

God was doing a new thing in our marriage, too. Craig and I were learning how to share our emotions with each other, finding small moments to fully listen to each other's hearts.

One day, without any fanfare or warning, Craig walked into our apartment with a very short letter from the hospital's financial office.

It read, "This letter is to inform you that your account has been brought to a $0 balance and has been closed."

Our $60,000+ medical bill had been canceled. We called the hospital, believing it was a mistake. The woman on the other end of the phone line said very unceremoniously, "The letter is accurate. Your account has been closed."

It was another modern-day miracle in our midst.

NO LONGER
BOUND

One Sunday morning in the new year, I heard an announcement at our church for a ministry called "No Longer Bound." It was a 14-week Bible study for men and women who have gone through the pain of an abortion and/or miscarriage.

In my heart, I knew I was supposed to sign up for it. The announcement continued, "This ministry provides a safe place for spiritual healing and deliverance through Jesus Christ to women and men who have been emotionally wounded by abortion and/or miscarriage."

I had heard the announcement for this Bible study the year before, but I felt like I was doing fine at that time and didn't need to open old wounds. After all, I had been in therapy for a while. I was already comforting countless women who had gone through miscarriages, as well as a few friends who had confided in me about their abortions.

Little did I know that "being just fine" was a ceiling, and God wanted it to become my floor. Fine and thriving are two different things.

Those private moments with these women made me realize how similar the emotions of losing a child can be. Whether it was an abortion, miscarriage, or even stillbirth, it didn't matter. It was the loss of a child that unified us. I realized that as I shared my story, it gave other women the courage to share their stories, too.

My friends who had confided in me their regret over abortions, along with my friends who had expressed their regret over their bodies failing them in a miscarriage, all had one thing in common. We all felt trapped in our circumstances. Each of us felt we should have done something different to change the outcome. We all felt powerless and full of pain, anger, and sadness toward our bodies, our friends, and our God.

Sitting in a room with women who had lost children—no matter the way—made sense to me. It was as if the Lord had been preparing my heart for years to hold the stories of babies who died too young. I was ready for the next layer of healing.

My new pastor's wife unknowingly helped me get ready for this group. She introduced me to Brené Brown's research on shame and vulnerability.

While sitting on her couch, I practiced taking my mask off. To my surprise, I was never shamed for having emotions. I couldn't believe the stories that were coming out of my mouth, the stories I had not shared with anyone in years. I jokingly told her that her tea must have truth serum in it.

My foolish vow to never accept guidance from a pastor was slowly revoked as my trust was building in the safety of her home.

If I could open up to one person, I could choose courage and open up to a group of people again.

A few weeks later, I found myself at our church offices, sitting in a room with eight other women. Apparently, no men had signed up for this year's study. As I was invited to share my story of infertility, miscarriages, and miracle babies, I allowed myself to share openly, without any buffers or concern that I would receive backlash or religious bypassing of emotions.

The facilitators, Chloe and Marianne, were trained in holding space for our tears. I could feel the warmth in their voices and in their body language as I expressed anger out loud, for the first time in a very long time.

Anger at my former pastor's wife for saying that maybe I wasn't meant to have children.

Anger at all the other lies thrown my way over the years by the older church ladies in my previous church.

The lie that my only value to society was to produce children.

The lie that maybe the reason I couldn't get pregnant was that I planned to continue to work outside the home.

All those toxic lies from years earlier came to the surface, creating bitterness in my mouth. I didn't even know I was still carrying pain from their words until this Bible study.

Forgiveness comes in layers.

As I continued to show up week after week, the

pain and anger slowly melted away, making a way for new hope. There was power in being invited to share the story of my hiding hope each week.

Hiding the hope that I would be a mama. Hiding the hope that pain and darkness wouldn't be the end of my story. Hiding the hope that my worth and identity were far beyond what my body could produce. Hiding the hope that Jesus would heal me—physically, mentally, emotionally, and spiritually.

I was learning that God uses what has harmed me to heal me. Being so open with the church ladies in our previous little church made me build walls around my heart. Being open in No Longer Bound made me dismantle those walls one brick at a time.

As my walls were coming down, I was learning to trust women again with the fragile parts of my heart. Vulnerability was key. The redemption of sitting in a circle with women and sharing my experiences without being offered religious advice or being interrupted was healing.

On the other hand, as great as the Bible study was, I was getting overwhelmed being there. Confronting trauma was grueling. I felt like I was digging up skeletons that had no place in my life but were somehow invisibly tied to my back. I thought I had already processed the pain, only to discover that the pain had simply been layered. Each layer defined how I interacted with others in the world.

Recognizing the cognitive dissonance was exhausting. Healing from it was invigorating.

Halfway through the 14 weeks, I was walking the grounds of the college campus the church offices were on, talking to the Lord.

Just heal me already!

I was done with the healing journey, only halfway into the Bible study. I just wanted to be healed. Now.

It was the week of my tenth baby's due date. With each miscarriage, due dates represented a release of heavy grief for me and a burden lifted from my heart.

As I walked, I silently begged Jesus to take all of the pain away—not just some of it, but all of it. Forever.

I don't want to continue living like this, always riding a roller coaster of emotions, never knowing when I will be triggered into anguish again.

Desperate for healing, I felt like I was the woman in Luke 8, bleeding for 12 years, desperately reaching to touch Jesus' garments. She spent her last coin trying to find a cure. No doctor could heal her, and yet, with one touch of the hem of Jesus' cloak, she was instantly healed. Her faith made her well.

As I was praying, I saw a tall woman wearing an African print dress walking towards me on the sidewalk. She looked like she had an ethereal light surrounding her entire body. It was as if she were walking out of the secret place of intimacy with the Father and right into my life.

I wanted to stop her and ask her to pray for me. I knew beyond a shadow of a doubt that she was a follower of Jesus. The glow around her was the exact same glow I had seen on Craig's face years earlier when he climbed the mountain.

I stared at her as she walked towards me. The Lord said to my spirit, *"This is the woman who founded No Longer Bound. When she prays for you, I will heal you."*

I was so stunned that the Lord told me who she was that when she stopped and asked me for directions to the church office, I could barely bring myself to point her in the right direction.

She continued her way across the campus. Roughly ten minutes later, I entered the church office where our session was held. Sure enough, I turned the corner to see the same woman I met on the sidewalk.

She looked shocked and said, "Oh, I just met you downstairs on the sidewalk," to which I eloquently replied with a nod, "Yep."

I was still trying to process the fact that, for the first time in my life, the Lord told me who a stranger was AND that I was going to be healed. HEALED. I knew I would not just survive—but thrive.

My hope was no longer hidden.

Psalm 147:3 — "He heals the brokenhearted and binds up their wounds."

It turned out the woman on the sidewalk was named Tegra Little. She founded the non-profit ministry, No Longer Bound, out of obedience to the Holy Spirit. She spent the evening sharing her testimony about her own journey.

In many ways, I felt a connection with her. I felt her confidence that each person who would go through No Longer Bound would be set free from their pain, and this sparked a renewed hope in my heart.

That night, Tegra mentioned that No Longer Bound holds biannual weekend healing retreats for men and women who have experienced the pain of abortion and/or miscarriage. I knew I needed to figure out a way to get there.

At the end of the evening, I was disappointed to see Tegra leave. I knew there was so much more to her story. The Lord told me if she prayed for me, He would heal me, but we didn't have prayer time that night. Still, something inside of me knew it wouldn't be the last time I saw her.

I arrived home, still shocked by my encounter with Tegra on the sidewalk. I told Craig that I would love for him to go with me to the retreat, but that I was going whether or not he came. I was desperate for healing. According to Craig, he heard, "You're going with me."

RETREAT

A couple weeks later, at a retreat center in Los Angeles, Craig and I sat in a large circle. There were 18 participants—men and women who desired for God to move in mighty ways and for Him to free each of us from shame, pain, and grief.

We walked up to the check-in table. A woman almost jumped out of her chair when she heard our names. Her love for the Lord exuded from her being and flowed right onto us.

The NLB leadership team looked like spiritual giants walking around the retreat grounds. I could *see* their faith in how each team member held such confidence in the Lord as they talked. I knew this team was a praying team.

I had never met a group of Christians so powerful and expectant in their prayers—in their battle cries for healing and deliverance. It was exhilarating to be in a room with such strong prayer warriors.

Once inside the room, each participant was invited to share their name and how they heard about No Longer Bound. I became more and more excited that the Holy Spirit was about to show Himself to me in a new way.

It felt possible for me to walk away from death and into a new life. Hope was rising that I would leave healed. 100% healed.

When it was Craig's turn to share, he said, "I heard of NLB through my wife, and at first I thought I was coming to support her, but I guess God has plans for me, too." He started to get teary-eyed, and the room went wild, acknowledging his bravery in coming to experience healing for himself.

I didn't realize he needed healing because of how quickly he seemed to recover from each of our miscarriages. It was news to me.

Throughout each session that weekend, I continued to experience new layers of healing. Indescribable healing. My hope was front and center.

Each time I heard my husband speak, I felt a new connection to his heart. Each time I saw him open up just a bit more with someone around him, I realized how distant we had been. I didn't realize how much I needed him on this journey that had spanned 13 years of our marriage.

After dinner one night, a man named Brother Charles, who was on the leadership team, made his way over to me.

He said, "You know, Linni, you shared about being upset that God answers your prayers for other women who have experienced infertility, and they get pregnant, but that you haven't gotten pregnant since your last miscarriage."

"Yes..." I replied cautiously, not knowing where

this was going.

Am I about to get a religious slap with a scripture verse attached?

"You know that you're anointed to heal women from infertility? God stored up all of your prayers in believing for your own children to come, and now when you pray, those prayer bowls get poured out on those women. It's your anointing." I was stunned.

> *Revelation 5:8b — "Each one had a harp and they were holding golden bowls full of incense, which are the prayers of God's people."*

The lens of trauma fell from my eyes. The world became brighter. I had never considered that the Lord was still using all of my prayers spoken over the last 13 years to now be the answer to someone else's prayers.

Later that night, Craig and I decided we needed guidance in making some decisions about our family's future. It was clear that Tegra and her husband, Pastor Marc, had a well-seasoned faith. We could trust them with our hearts. *Redemption.*

We sat down at midnight. It had been a long day of ministry, and yet, they were willing to stay up late to pray for us.

I asked, "What does life look like for us after this weekend? Do we keep trying to expand our family? We're unclear about our next steps." The turmoil of indecision whirled around me as I spoke.

Tegra and Pastor Marc prayed over us. Pastor Marc sensed that I was dreaming old dreams and that God wanted to give me new dreams to dream.

That prayer and insight touched me to the core, cutting the turmoil. The timing of that word was spot on. If it had been said even a few months earlier, I would not have been ready to hear it. God always knows what we need and when we need it. My spirit lifted.

Okay, God! I'm clay in your hands! What new dreams do you have for me?

On the last day of the Weekend Healing Retreat, No Longer Bound hosted a Celebration of Life service in the chapel of the retreat center, where participants were given an opportunity to honor their babies.

Craig and I stood up at the podium as a couple, saying the names of each of our babies—the names Mikayla and Victoria chose for their siblings. Craig started sobbing as he spoke. My heart grew three sizes watching him bravely share his story—a story that I had only ever seen glimpses of.

When it was my turn to speak, I turned to my husband and said words that I had not planned on saying but that unexpectedly came out of my mouth, "Craig, you can stop beating yourself up. I forgive you for not always being there for me. I would do it all over again knowing that you would be by my side now."

I felt as if we had just exchanged wedding vows.

I heard an audible "wow" from the audience, and, with that, I interpreted the song, "His Eye is on the Sparrow," into ASL as a dedication to our babies.

I had asked another participant to sing the song a

cappella for me. It was my way of honoring our babies. God had been watching them all along. Having someone else sing was a symbol that many friends had been invited along for our journey. His eye had truly been on us all along.

Pastor Marc gave a message about not leaving with our grave clothes still on. Remembering what the therapist had said to me almost three years earlier, it resonated with me deeply.

Would I allow my grief and trauma, carrying the stench of death, to clothe me a second longer? Or would I allow God to renew my life on a new path of hope?

I decided right then and there that my last few layers of grave clothes would not accompany me home.

In my spirit, I saw dirty, mud-streaked linens being lifted off my shoulders. My identity was no longer in my pain, but in the healing power of my Lord and Savior, Jesus Christ.

I recalled what the Lord had said a few weeks earlier, and I knew it to be true: *"When she prays for you, I will heal you."*

Luke 4:18-19 — "The Spirit of the Lord is on me, because he has anointed me to proclaim good news to the poor. He has sent me to proclaim freedom for the prisoners and recovery of sight for the blind, to set the oppressed free, to proclaim the year of the Lord's favor."

I was walking out healed and I would continue to heal. If I allow God to mold me as clay in His hands, His work is never finished.

At the end of the service, Craig and I turned toward each other. My hope for a new beginning was high. We held hands and walked out the chapel doors, hoping to never be the same again. It was time to thrive.

New
Beginnings

After the Weekend Healing Retreat, I kept expecting Craig and me to turn back to our old ways of disconnecting. But Craig didn't turn away from me; he continued to turn towards me. I slowly started to realize how far apart we had been because of how close we were becoming.

As if we were newlyweds experiencing each other for the first time, we were learning to share in each other's joy and sadness, hopes and new dreams. We were learning to trust one another so that when one of us fell, the other would be there to pick them up.

The new dream of becoming best friends with my husband was coming true. We were in awe of all that God had done. He was finally seeing me, and I, him. *Restoration.*

The NLB Bible study still had a few weeks left after the retreat was held. One of the participants mentioned microchimerism to me one night as we were walking to our cars.

Microchimerism is the presence of tiny cells from the baby still in the mother's body. When I heard this term, I finally understood why I felt like our dining room table was missing people, because "...bone of my bones and flesh of my flesh" from Genesis 2 was real.

I was truly missing family members around my table. It made sense why I desired to have more children, especially around my table, because I was genuinely missing my children that I had miscarried. It was a normal reaction to my circumstances. I wanted them to be home with me.

Genesis 2:23a — "...bone of my bones and flesh of my flesh..."

Roughly a month after the No Longer Bound Weekend Healing Retreat, the No Longer Bound Bible study had their own Celebration of Life Ceremony.

It was springtime, and I was finally ready to write a letter to my children. I deeply desired to honor each of their lives and the place they will always hold in my heart. Reading my letter about our journey of hiding hope in the midst of infertility, miscarriages, and miracle babies in front of other women who had lost children too was an even greater level of healing. There was purpose in my journey, to let others know that He never leaves us nor forsakes us in our deepest pain.

After we each read our letters to our children, we released one dove for each child not on this earth. My hope was no longer in hiding, but on full display for all to see. The oil of gladness covered me. Craig and I held eight doves, releasing them together. Each dove flew high in the sky, trained to go home. My babies were Home.

And as for me, *I am no longer bound.*

> *Psalm 23:6 — "Surely your goodness*
> *and love will follow me all the days*
> *of my life, and I will dwell in the*
> *house of the Lord forever."*

Remembering the books I had read on infertility and miscarriages more than a decade earlier, that weren't comforting at the time, they were actually right:

"Miscarriages are hard,

...but God is good."

A LETTER TO MY CHILDREN

Dear Claire, Mia, Daniel, Aurora, Gavin, Alyssa, Dylan, and Noelle,

Words don't seem to do you honor or show you how much you are loved.

I have told our testimony like this: "I've told my husband ten times, 'We're pregnant!' We've had eight miscarriages and two miracle babies!" as if the two miracle babies erase eight little Weishaars running around Heaven.

I knew it was socially taboo to talk about miscarriages with you, Claire, so only a few of your family members knew about you, but none of our friends.

But, when I was pregnant with you, Mia, I knew I wanted as many people to pray for me as possible, and I didn't care who knew. I wanted to fill up those bowls of prayers in Heaven.

But, I quickly learned that my tears after losing you made others feel uncomfortable. My tears even made ME feel uncomfortable. I believed I needed to get over you quickly, because I didn't know how to handle my own pain. So, I quickly buried you in my mind. After all, I had hope against hope that we would have children.

Then, Daniel, you came, and no heartbeat was found. I still had morning sickness with you as we waited for you to be released. I judged myself for crying, for having emotion. I had no clue this was grief or loss at the time. Even so, when the doctor said we would have a ten percent chance of ever having children, my spirit jumped within me, and I laughed, saying, "Oh, Jesus loves those kinds of numbers!"

The next day I was devastated, but a friend called to tell me, "You can't believe what those doctors said. You are going to have a baby." She didn't know about the diagnosis or you, Daniel. We believed that word. We picked the name "Mikayla" because we were going to praise the Lord for a baby that was not yet born, but yet to come.

Then, Aurora, you came a year later, and I was put on bedrest. I had so much faith that you were going to make it. I just KNEW you were coming.

But, then, you went to be in the arms of Jesus. That summer was the closest I had been to the Lord. It was a bittersweet time. I knew Jesus had me. I knew THIS was a part of my testimony of God's faithfulness, and yet I couldn't understand why the desire to be a mama ran so deep if that couldn't happen. His word was a lamp unto my feet and a light unto my path.

Then we thought we found out what was wrong, and surgery on my uterus was done. And six weeks later, your sister, Mikayla Hope, was conceived, and our arms were full. We were done trying for any more children and were completely content with her.

However, unexpectedly, we found out that you, Gavin, were within my womb, and the excitement that you were coming filled our hearts with so much joy! There wasn't an ounce of worry. After all, your sister was here. But, then, you slipped away before we could say "baby," back into the Father's arms. Then I learned that this pain is called grief and loss.

Grief and loss became my companions. Oh, Jesus was still good, but I lived with masks on, pretending I was okay, or that each of you were just events of a baby lifted to Jesus, or better yet, just a dream lost, never to be found.

Then, the Holy Spirit whispered in my ear—the only time I have ever heard the audible voice of the Lord—"Her name will be Victoria Faith." I was immediately overjoyed! We were promised another baby!

Your daddy came home from work that night and told me, "The Lord told me the name of our next baby!" Really? What? "Victoria Faith."

A month later, we found out we were pregnant, and of course we knew this was Victoria, but it turns out this was you, Alyssa. You were the boldness that we needed to declare God's word, and this is where our story no longer made sense to me. After six miscarriages and one miracle baby, why would this be our story?

Our fertility specialist shook his head and scratched his brow. With an empathetic voice, he said, "I thought I fixed this!" And I said, "Only God can fix me." With that, Secondary Unexplained Infertility was written into my records. But God had other plans.

Almost a year later, we found out we were pregnant with you, Dylan. Your name means "Steadfast in Christ." We just gave up our house and had no clue where the next dollar was going to come from, and to be pregnant with you was such a sign of Christ's steadfast faithfulness. Yet, you never made it to this earth; you only knew of Heaven.

THEN, we heard the most beautiful sound in the world. Victoria Faith was coming. Many people prayed for you, and we shouted that God is Victoriously Faithful.

My heart was full—two MIRACLE babies, what a life! But, in the back recesses of my mind, anger was building. Landmines were hidden. Unexpected passersby received the wrath of my concealed anger.

One misstep and BOOM, friendships dissolved, our own DREAMS shattered, and my relationship with your daddy began to become more and more distant, as he didn't know how to handle my outbursts, and I didn't know why I was becoming such an angry person.

"Why can't I just move one? Why am I stuck in the trenches? Why can't I see the light of day?"

How was I to mourn you when I only knew of each of you for a few seconds? It didn't seem logical to me. Yet, I unknowingly started living as if someone forgot to bury me. But, in all reality, I have worn grave clothes for many years, not knowing how to get rid of the stench of my own rotting heart.

In the recent years I have learned to take the mask off, I have learned to not respond with the socially acceptable responses, but to say what needs to be said in order for me to be set free.

You have many friends in Heaven whose mamas come to me often for comfort. I have learned how to comfort those who also wear sackcloth, but I didn't know how my mourning would ever turn into true-lasting dancing. I couldn't wrap my head around this.

After you, Noelle, my heart stopped beating this past summer, and I raised my white flag in surrender. You are the reason I came to No Longer Bound, where the Lord gave me peace.

I've heard it said, that you don't just lose a dream, you lose the first of everything. The first time you smile, the first time you crawl, and the first time you walk. The first time you say, "Mama."

As your sisters began to grow, I started to miss you more and more. When I set the dinner table, it felt so empty, and I didn't know why. I thought if I just had another child, that emptiness would go away, but I learned, too, that that is a lie.

Now, I know that each of you have a place and purpose in eternity. Your names are telling of that. Your names tell of our journey on this earth with the Lord.

Imagine our surprise when, just a few weeks ago, your sisters named you, and we saw the thread of God's faithfulness in the naming of each of you.

Claire—He is Bright
Mia—Bitterly Wanted Child
Daniel—God is My Judge
Aurora—God is My Mouthpiece
Gavin—God made me Content
Alyssa—God made me Bold

Dylan—God made me Steadfast in Christ
Noelle—God gave me Peace

He has been gracious to me in that I have seen your faces in a vision. Your sisters love you and miss you. Mikayla and Victoria ask about you all the time. I don't always know what to say to them about you, but I believe the Lord will show me.

The Lord has been gracious to me and has shown me each of you playing around my rocking chair that was bought to remember His promises never fail.

Because of No Longer Bound, I realize each of you are bone of my bones and flesh of my flesh. You cannot be replaced. Oddly enough, this gives me peace.

I carried you every second of your life, and I will love you for every second of mine.

Love,

Your Mama

WHEN THERE'S
DEATH IN THE FAMILY

When a friend's family member dies, you send cards, make dinner, give them some space, or smother them with love and your time. You attend a funeral, wear black, tell stories, and if you have had a close family member die, too, you understand their grief in a way that no one else ever could.

What I didn't know is that each miscarriage is a death. A death of a dream of a colorful nursery, a death of breastfeeding a little one, a death of being called "Mama", a death of a soul—and my own death of hope.

I knew what I was experiencing was sadness, but I didn't really understand that sadness until my own mama passed away. Because of her unexpected death, my grief lingered on my grave clothes. It was only after a period of intense grief for my mama that I realized the sadness of a miscarriage was really a grieving process over my unborn baby's death.

A letter I wrote to a friend after I heard of her miscarriage was everything I wished someone would have told me when I was miscarrying our babies:

Dearly Beloved,

I'm so sorry that you've lost your baby. I'm sitting here just sobbing for you. My heart breaks for you. I understand your grief. You are not alone. Even if it seems as if no one truly understands, lean and press into our Father, who lost His Son.

Pressing in may feel difficult, but there are so many rewards in leaning into His hands. Your heavenly Father is close and His comfort is a warm blanket on a cold, snowy day. Let Him cover you with His warm embrace and His everlasting love.

I could never understand why the grief felt so deep, why the pain felt so great. I knew God was good, I knew things would work out for His glory, but I never quite understood my emotions with losing a baby I never held, until I lost my mom.

It was as if God was telling me that I was allowed to experience a deep sorrow and that didn't mean that my faith was rocked. The grief of losing a loved one, and the grief of losing a baby you never held, is the same exact feeling, the only difference is the memories.

Grief is grief. You now have a piece of Heaven. Your baby will never experience the pains of this world and yet will greet you one day when you walk through those pearly gates!

Jesus gets to rock that baby for you. May you continue to be lifted up in your time of sorrow, and may you see the graciousness of the One who truly knows how to comfort you.

May you not be hard on yourself for the

emotions you experience. May you not rush your own healing process but allow Jesus to hold you. May you lift up your tears to Him.

Know you are loved,

Linni

AN APOLOGY

If your arms are empty and you have been hurt intentionally or unintentionally by friends, family, colleagues, and/or church members who did not know what to say when you were hurting, on behalf of the body of Christ, I ask, will you forgive me for hurting you?

When stupid comments were said when you were losing your baby.

When empty platitudes of false encouragement were offered while you had tears streaming down your face.

When you were never given closure, I want to stand in the gap and say to you, "I'm so sorry."

I did not support you.

I shamed you.

I turned my back.

I said the wrong thing at the wrong time.

I did not love you the way you needed to be loved.

I did not hug you.

I did not sit in silence with you.

I did not say, "I'm so sorry."

You deserved better from me. I apologize for not acknowledging your broken heart. I apologize for not being there for you physically, emotionally, and mentally during your greatest pain and in your darkest hour.

Will you forgive me?

A PRAYER

Lord, I pray for couples who have broken marriages due to infertility and/or child loss. I declare that their hearts be mended in Your loving arms, Father.

I pray for a deep connection to take place between husband and wife as they learn how to love each other in the midst of uncertainty and despair. I pray for words to be forgiven that have been spoken out of pain.

Jesus, I ask for You to come in and show them where you have been in the midst of their heartache; show them where you are right in the middle of their grieving.

Give them a fresh revelation of how you care for them. That you are with them and for them. That you will never leave them nor forsake them. That you desire for their marriage to be made whole. Your design for marriages is for it to thrive. We pray for their marriage to thrive, Lord. May their marriage be a testimony that you make all things new.

For those who desire the miracle of a child in their arms, Lord, would you show up for them? I declare that the curse of death will not define their destiny.

That the enemy, whose assignment is to steal, kill, and destroy, is defeated by the blood of the Lamb and the word of their testimony.

Lord, I declare life over wombs that have been graveyards for unborn babies. I declare that the pain of an infertility diagnosis will not be the end of their story. I declare that the pain and shame of losing a child from a failed adoption, miscarriage, or abortion to be redeemed.

Would you make empty arms full? Would you make a way where there is no way, Lord?

I declare a renewed sense of hope and faith in their weary souls. I declare a sound mind and courageous faith to take hold.

Give them a vision for their future that surpasses all understanding, knowing that you are the author and perfecter of life.

I declare that the blood of Jesus Christ is on you to heal you and deliver you from the torment of the enemy. That your hope will be in the God who still does miracles today.

In Jesus name I pray, Amen!

(Revelation 21:5, Deuteronomy 31:6, Romans 4:17b, John 10:10, Revelation 12:11, Acts 3:15)

Healing our communities
one trauma at a time

No Longer Bound

Abortion | Miscarriage Recovery Ministry

Have you or anyone you know been affected by abortion and/or miscarriage?
The physical and emotional stress can be devastating and often surfaces months
or even years later.

ABOUT

No Longer Bound Abortion | Miscarriage
Recovery Ministry provides a safe place
for spiritual healing and deliverance
through Jesus Christ to women and men
who have been emotionally wounded by
abortion and/or miscarriage.

MINISTRY OPPORTUNITIES

- 14-Week Bible Study - Recovery Groups

- A 3-Day Weekend Retreat

- Discipleship Groups

- Donate- The services No Longer
  Bound provides are possible only
  through the generosity of our
  prayer partners, volunteer
  facilitators, and the financial
  contributions of individuals,
  churches, and organizations.

SYMPTOMS :

- Guilt
- Shame
- Sorrow
- Grief
- Anger
- Rage
- Anxiety
- Depression
- Suicidal thoughts
- Eating disorders
- Drug and alcohol abuse
- Difficulty with relationships
- Sexual dysfunction
- Emotional numbness
- Bouts of crying
- Loneliness
- Spiritual isolation
- Lowered self-esteem
- Trouble sleeping
- Nightmares or flashbacks
- Discomfort around babies or
  pregnant women

CONTACT NLB

INFO@NOLONGERBOUNDMINISTRY.ORG
WWW.NOLONGERBOUNDMINISTRY.ORG

Resources

Websites:

No Longer Bound
www.NoLongerBoundMinistry.org

Rachel's Vineyard
www.RachelsVineyard.org

Rachel's Gift
www.Rachelsgift.org

Linni Weishaar
www.LinniWeishaar.com

Jewish Periods of Mourning
www.shiva.com/learning-center/
understanding/periods-of-mourning/

BOOKS:

Daring Greatly: How the Courage to Be Vulnerable Transforms the Way We Live, Love, Parent, and Lead by Brené Brown

When God & Grief Meet: Comfort and Courage for Your Journey by Lynn Eib

Inner Healing and Deliverance Handbook: Hope to Bring Your Heart Back to Life by Jennifer Eivaz

Suffering Is Never for Nothing by Elisabeth Elliot

When Faith Meets Therapy: Find Hope and a Practical Path to Emotional, Spiritual, and Relational Healing by Anthony Evans

Defeating Strongholds of the Mind: A Believer's Guide to Breaking Free by Rebecca Greenwood

No Longer Bound: The Unborn Children by Tegra Little

According to Your Word Lord, I Pray by Louis McCall

Hannah's Hope: Seeking God's Heart in the Midst of Infertility, Miscarriage, and Adoption Loss by Jennifer Saake

Emotionally Healthy Spirituality: It's Impossible to Be Spiritually Mature, While Remaining Emotionally Immature by Peter Scazzero

Healing the Wounded Soul: Break Free from the Pain of the Past and Live again by Katie Souza

Beside Still Waters: Words of Comfort for the Soul by Charles H. Spurgeon

The Pursuit of God by A.W. Tozer

Where Is God When It Hurts/What's So Amazing About Grace? by Philip Yancey

ACKNOWLEDGEMENTS

It is more difficult and more fulfilling than I could have ever anticipated to pour my heart and soul into the pages of this book. Without my husband and best friend, Craig, none of this would have been possible.

You stayed up late into the night editing concepts and adding scripture references that needed to bless the reader and me.

Pastor Craig, you have become my ride or die in every ounce of our lives together since that fateful day at No Longer Bound. I am so grateful to the Lord for the redemption of our marriage and our dreams. You are my biggest fan, and I, yours. Here's to dreaming new dreams together, my love!

Thank you to Rachel Pastukhov, who many moons ago noticed a 19-year-old girl who had a twinkle in her eye for Craig Weishaar. I am forever grateful for your matchmaking endeavor.

Over the course of the last 20 plus years of our friendship, you have been in my corner through it all. You have let me talk your ear off for decades without complaint.

You answered phone calls at 3:00 a.m. when I was

miscarrying. You let me weep tears of joy over pregnancies. You prayed powerful prayers of intercession and reminded me of God's promises when I could not hold on any longer.

You labored with me in this book by recounting stories I had long forgotten and helping me with all my run-on sentences.

Thank you to Letica Perez, for asking me deep, thought-provoking questions that helped me share this story to its fullest potential. Without your constant nudging, asking me when I would ever finish *Hiding Hope*, I don't know if this book would have left my computer and made its way into the hands of readers.

To our shared love of Brené Brown and large cups of coffee, you have taught me to be vulnerable and open in visiting arenas, like writing again.

Thank you to Rachel Rasmussen, for listening to my heart when I said I desired to write *Hiding Hope*, but I had no clue where to begin. There are no words to truly express my gratitude for the gift of time you gave me during this publishing journey.

Thank you to Gwen Gibson, for helping me process elements of my life and thus this book aloud. I am blessed to see your love for the Lord on full display even during 9:00 p.m. chats over tea. One day we'll get to Israel together!

Thank you to Katie and Daniel Weishaar, for loving us through the thick and thin of this storm of infertility.

Thank you to Foster and Michelle Brereton, for your love and encouragement during the hard years of

never knowing if we would have children and believing right along with us that we would have babies
in our arms. Thank you for your friendship that surpassed understanding.

Thank you to Bethany Baird, for teaching me that
being a woman of God was a much greater calling than
only being a mother of children on all of our treks up
therapy mountain.

Thank you to Laura Thomas, for staying with me
the day I heard the news that my mama had passed
away. You became a mother to me in many ways by
offering so much comfort and love during our miscarriages after her passing.

Thank you to Matt and Vicky Dunn, for allowing
me to sit on your couch as I practiced taking my mask
off while processing my journey. You sowed a seed that
is now flourishing.

Thank you to Papa Ché and Mama Sue, for
partnering with No Longer Bound. Your "yes" to this
ministry forever changed our lives. Thank you for
running to me every time you saw me.

Thank you to Tegra Little, for being obedient to
the Holy Spirit in creating a safe place for me to heal
within the walls of No Longer Bound. If it was not for
NLB, I do not know where I would be. Thank you for
your prayers of deliverance in my life and your
constant love. You are a mother to a motherless
generation.

Thank you to Pastor Marc Little, my Spiritual
Father, for covering Craig and me in every aspect of
our lives. You not only have taught us what a pastor's
covering feels like, but you have taught us to laugh in

the face of the enemy. When a weapon is formed against us it shall not prosper! Your friendship has healed many wounds.

Last, but not least, thank you to the No Longer Bound Leadership Team past and present: Sandi Adams, Candace Aikin, Christian Bradley, Sebrina Brooks, Debra Calloway, Lisa Carter, Marianne Castillo, Debbie Chandler, Jade Clarke, Kimberley Cornell, Dr. Lucien Cox, Charles De Cuir,

Jackie D'Meza, Anthony Fields, Dr. Rodney Foster, Angela Franklin, Angela Giles, Chloe Gitelson, Arianna Hernandez, Eleen Hupf, Shannon Jackson, Trecia Johnson, Dr. Roxanne Jordan, Dr. Linda Marcell, Tanis Matthews,

Allison and David Medley, Christina Munoz, Terri O'Callaghan, Jacqueline Redeemer, Lisa Ridgeway, Patricia Roach, Elestine Smittick, Gloria Stoop, Sondra White, Alesa Williams, Joyce Zenon-Peters, and Patti Young.

I have never seen a group of people more dedicated to walking with each other in the day-to-day life than this team. Each of you truly embody Isaiah 61:1:

"The Spirit of the Sovereign LORD is on me, because the LORD has anointed me to proclaim good news to the poor. He has sent me to bind up the brokenhearted, to proclaim freedom for the captives and release from darkness for the prisoners."

I love you all. It is an honor to know you and serve right alongside you.

ABOUT THE AUTHOR

Linni Weishaar is a retired superhero. As an educator and teacher for the last 18 years, her greatest joy is helping other women find healing and wholeness in their life stories.

She and her husband currently serve on the leadership team of No Longer Bound, a ministry that provides a safe place for spiritual healing and deliverance through Jesus Christ to women and men who have been emotionally wounded by abortion and/or miscarriage.

After spending many years in a little town called Los Angeles, she found a new home in the California mountains, where she lives with her husband, two miracle babies, and her Golden Retriever.

You can find Linni on
Instagram @hiding.hope

www.LinniWeishaar.com

or send her an email at
info@hidinghope.org

Has Linni's journey touched your heart?
Please consider leaving a review on
Amazon, Goodreads, or Barnes & Noble
so that others can hear her story, too.

.

Made in the USA
Middletown, DE
16 August 2023